The Power of the Penne

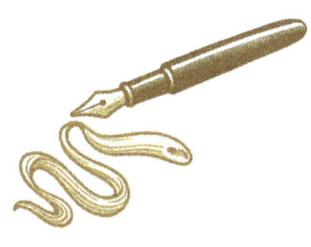

Write
Choice
Ink
ESTABLISHED 2021

POWER OF THE PENNE

Lovingly Curated Handwritten Recipes

ISBN:978-1-970181-61-6
First Edition — 2025
Printed in the United States of America

Disclaimer:
The publisher and contributors have made every effort to ensure the accuracy and safety of the recipes contained herein. However, results may vary depending on ingredients, equipment, and individual cooking methods. The publisher and contributors assume no responsibility for accidents, allergic reactions, or outcomes resulting from the preparation or consumption of these recipes. Always follow safe food-handling practices.

Published by Write Choice Ink Ventura, California, 2025

Dedication

A tribute to the cooks, mothers fathers, family, and friends who left us their best food with their best handwriting. Let's try the recipes and analyze the writing too.

Tricia Clapp

Foreword

The idea for this cookbook began as a simple thought: how wonderful it would be to gather recipes from colleagues and friends around the world—people connected not just through handwriting, but through shared curiosity, creativity, and community. When I asked for contributions, the response was immediate and enthusiastic. Recipes started arriving in my inbox—some treasured family favorites, others inventive new creations—all handwritten with the familiar, personal touch.

Each contributor offered one or several recipes across a variety of categories, and together, created something far richer than I could have imagined: a collection that celebrates both individuality and connection, taste and tradition, the written word and the shared meal. The comments, unless otherwise noted, belong to the contributor.

The book's title, *The Power of the Penne*, was inspired by the AHAF anthology I edited a few years ago–*The Power of the Pen*. One of our clever members, Anthony Brochetelli—who generously contributed several delicious Italian recipes—suggested this playful twist on the name.

It perfectly captured the spirit of the project: equal parts creativity, humor, and heart.

The recipes are accompanied by photographs, most images royalty-free art chosen to *represent* the dish rather than attempt to depict it exactly as it appears when prepared. The focus of this book is the handwritten page and the personal stories behind it—the human touch that turns a simple recipe into a shared experience.

A nonprofit educational organization founded in 1967, the American Handwriting Analysis Foundation (AHAF), is dedicated to the study and appreciation of handwriting as a key to understanding human expression. While not all of those who sent recipes are members, this book reflects that mission, celebrating not only the artistry of the written word but also the connections it creates among people everywhere.

The Power of the Penne is a testament to what can happen when an international community comes together, blending its diverse flavors and talents into one warm, nourishing whole. My gratitude goes to everyone who participated, stirred, baked, seasoned, and shared a piece of themselves on these pages.

— Sheila Lowe
Editor & Compiler

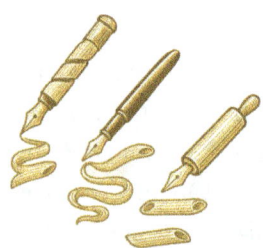

www.ahafhandwriting.org

Table of Contents

Breads

Cakes

Cookies

Pies

Desserts

Main Dishes

Side Dishes

Soups and Sauces

Salads & Vegetable Dishes

Dips & Dressings

Beverages

Pumpkin Bread

INGREDIENTS

Wet

2 cups cooked pumpkin
1 cup salad oil
2/3 cup water
4 whole eggs, beaten

Dry

3 ½ cups flour
3 cups sugar
2 tsp baking soda
3 tsp cinnamon
1 ½ tsp salt
1 ½ tsp ginger
1 tsp cloves

DIRECTIONS

Combine wet ingredients together.
Make a well in dry ingredients, add pumpkin mixture and blend until smooth.
Add dates, raisins, nuts as desired–chop into pieces but not too small.
Pour into 2 well-greased and floured loaf pans.
Bake at 350 for 1 hour, 2 minutes, then test for doneness.

NOTES

Contributed by Ruth Holmes

Pumpkin Bread 350°
1 hr. 20 min

Dry —
- 3½ c. flour
- 3 C. sugar
- 2 tsp. soda
- 1½ tsp. salt
- 3 tsp. cinnamon
- 1½ tsp. ginger
- 1 tsp. cloves

Mix together

Another Bowl w/ Beater —
- 2 Cups Pumpkin
- 1 Cup Salad Oil
- 2/3 Cup water
- 4 whole eggs — beat well.

Make a well in dry ingredients + add pumpkin mix. Blend until smooth.

Add dates, raisins + nuts as desired. Pour into 2 loaf pans — well greased + floured.

Bake at 350°

After 1' 20 minutes Test w/ Tester for Doneness

chop nuts into small pieces but don't chop or make too small.

Enjoy!

from Pat Dalrick

3

Scotch Scones

INGREDIENTS

Wet

½ cup shortening
2 eggs, beaten
¼ cup milk

Dry

2 cups flour
½ cup sugar
½ cup raisins
2 tsp cream of tartar
1 tsp baking soda
¾ tsp salt

DIRECTIONS

Sift together the dry ingredients.
Blend with shortening to the consistency of breadcrumbs. Add remaining ingredients and blend with hands into a dough.
Divide into 3 parts, then flatten into ½ inch thick circles.
Use a pastry cutter to make four circles in each part.
Bake at 400 degrees for 15 minutes

NOTES

What people in the US call scones is quite different from English (or Scottish) ones. This recipe, by a 1970s chef, comes closer than most. And to be really English, you'll slather them with jam and whipped cream (in UK it's "clotted cream," which is closer to whipped butter.

Contributed by Sheila Lowe

Scotch Scones

Don Fitz

2 C flour
½ C sug.
2 t cream tartar ⎫ Sift.
1 t B.Soda
¾ t. Salt

Blend w. ½ C. Shortening til "Bread crumbs"

½ C raisins
2 eggs, beaten ⎫ add, mix
¼ C Milk ↓

Divide into 3, flatten into Circles ½" thick. Divid into 4's

400° — 15 mins

Mom's Stuffing

Ingredients

A loaf of stale bread

Onion, chopped

Celery, chopped

Thyme

Directions

Water down the bread and break it up
Fry the onion and celery in butter, add thyme to taste.
Mix all ingredients together and fry until drier.
Then stuff.

Notes

Contributed by Kathleen Dickinson

Recipe: Stuffing

From: mom   Makes:

water down bread
break it up
onion & celery fried in
butter   add thyme to taste
mix all together & fry
until drier
    then stuff

Crusty Cornbread

INGREDIENTS

Dry

1 cup self-rising flour
1 cup self-rising cornmeal

Wet

1 cup milk or
buttermilk
1 egg, beaten
¼ cup melted butter or
bacon drippings

DIRECTIONS

Mix dry ingredients with egg, milk, butter. Stir until
moistened. Pour into hot frying pan or square pan. Bake
at for 25 minutes at 425 degrees or until golden brown.

NOTES

Contributed by Lib Porter via Helene Robinson

HERE'S WHAT'S COOKING: Crusty Corn Bread
FROM THE KITCHEN OF: LIB PORTER PICKENS, SC

1 C. self-rising flour
1 C. " - " corn meal
1 Egg - beaten
1 C. milk - Buttermilk
¼ C. melted butter or bacon drippings

Mix dry ingredient with egg, milk, butter. Stir until moistened. Pour into hot fry pan or square pan. Bake at 425° for 25 min. or until golden brown.

Herb Bread

INGREDIENTS

Wet

1 pt milk, scalded
(powdered milk may be
substituted)
2 eggs, beaten

Dry

1 yeast cake
7-8 cups flour (more if
needed)
1 Tbsp salt
½ cup sugar
1 ½ tsp nutmeg
1 Tbsp nutmeg
1 Tbsp crumbled sage
1 Tbsp caraway

DIRECTIONS

None were given.

NOTES

Add a pinch of marjoram for joy, rosemary for health
and long life.
Makes 2 loaves

Contributed by Ruth Holmes

Herb Bread

1 yeast cake	7-8 c flour (more if needed)
1 pt milk, scalded	(powdered milk may be substituted for scalded milk)
1/4 c butter	
1 T salt	
1/2 c sugar	(pinch of marjoram for joy)
2 eggs, beaten	" " rosemary for health + long life
1 1/2 tsp nutmeg	
1 T crumbled sage	2 loaves
1 T caraway	

Butter Rolls

INGREDIENTS

Wet

2 cups lukewarm water (1
cup to dissolve yeast)
1 cup shortening
2 eggs

Dry

¾ cup sugar
2 tsp salt
3 cups flour (at least)
3 pkg yeast

DIRECTIONS

Mix shortening, sugar and salt until creamy. Add eggs
ONE AT A TIME while yeast is dissolving in 1 cup
water.

Add yeast and 2nd cup of water. Add 3 cups flour (at
least). Stir, continue adding flour (will use +/- 2 ½ lb of
flour or more).

Pat on floured bread board. Knead until it won't hold
flour anymore (from the board). Put in greased mixing
bowl. Grease the top of dough and prove. Let rise 3x at
least. Squeeze through hands and let rise again.

Bake at 350 deg. For 25-30 minutes

NOTES

Contributed by Peg Brantley

Butter Rolls

1 c Shortening	3 pckg yeast
3/4 c Sugar	2 c lukewarm
2 t salt	water (1 c to
2 eggs	dissolve yeast)
3 c flour (at least)	

Mix Shortening, Sugar & salt until
Creamy. Add eggs ONE AT A
TIME while yeast is dissolving
in 1 c of water. Add yeast

and 2nd c of water. Add 3 c
of flour (at least) Stir in
Continue adding flour (will
use ± 2½ lb of flour or more).
Pat on floured bread board. Knead
until it won't hold flour anymore
(from the board). Put in greased
mixing bowl. Grease the top of
dough. Let it rise 3X at least.
Squeeze through hands & let

rise again. Bake at 350°
for 25-30 min.

Pumpkin Muffins

INGREDIENTS

Wet

1 cup pumpkin
3 eggs
2/3 cup dry milk
½ c grated carrots
1 tsp vanilla

Dry

1 tsp pumpkin pie spice
1 tsp cinnamon
1 tsp baking soda
5 packets sweetener
6 tbsp flour

DIRECTIONS

Mix all ingredients together. Pour into muffin pan.
Bake at 350 for 10-12 minutes

NOTES

Contributed by Peg Brantley

CHECKS (LIST SINGLY)	DOLLARS	CENTS
1. Pumpkin Muffins		
2. 1 c. pumpkin		
3. 2 eggs		
4. 2/3 c. dry milk		
5. 1/2 c. carrots, grated		
6. 1/4 c. raisins		
7. 1 t. vanilla		
8. 2 t. pumpkin pie spice		
9. 1 t. cinnamon		
10. 1 t. bkng. soda		
11. 5 pkts. sweetener		
12. 1 c. flour		
13.		
14. Mix all ingredients.		
15. Pour in muffin pan.		
16. Bake at 350° for		
17. 10-12 minutes		
18.		

Gramma's White Bread

INGREDIENTS

Wet

1 quart warm water

Dry

1 pkg Carnation dried milk
¼ cup sugar
1/3 cup shortening (part lard, part bacon fat, melted)
14-16 cups flour

DIRECTIONS

It's assumed that all ingredients are mixed together.
Let rise until double in bulk.
Knead or cut into five sections.
Knead each section until smooth and place in buttered pans. Let rise (Ed. Note–until doubled in size?).
Bake at 350 deg. For 40 minutes

NOTES

Contributed by Ruth Holmes

Gramma's White Bread — 5 loaves

1 pkg Carnation dried milk   1/3
1/4 c sugar
4 tsp salt
1/2 cup shortning (part lard, part bacon fat, melted)

3 pkg. yeast
1 qt. warm water
14 -16 cups flour →

Let rise til double in bulk.
Knead + cut in five sections. Knead
each section til smooth + place in
buttered pans. Let rise. Bake 350° —
40'.

Pritikin Bran Muffins

INGREDIENTS

Wet

2 cups skim milk
½ cup apple juice
concentrate
½ tsp vanilla

¼ cup egg whites (about
4) - beat until stiff peaks
form

Dry

2 cups whole wheat flour
2 cups all bran cereal
1 tsp baking soda
½ tsp baking powder
½ tsp cinnamon
1/8 tsp nutmeg
1/8 tsp powdered cloves

DIRECTIONS

Combine dry ingredients in large bowl. Combine wet
ingredients in medium bowl (Ed. note: except egg whites,
which are beaten separately).
Mix the wet mixture into the dry mixture until smooth.
Fold in egg whites until mixture is uniform in textured.
Scoop into greased (I use Pam) muffin tins.
Bake 300-325 deg. For 25-30 minutes until puffed and
lightly browned on top. Makes 16-18 muffins.

NOTES

I use 1-1½ tsp baking powder and more spices than
suggested. I eliminate the nutmeg.

Contributed by Ruth Holmes

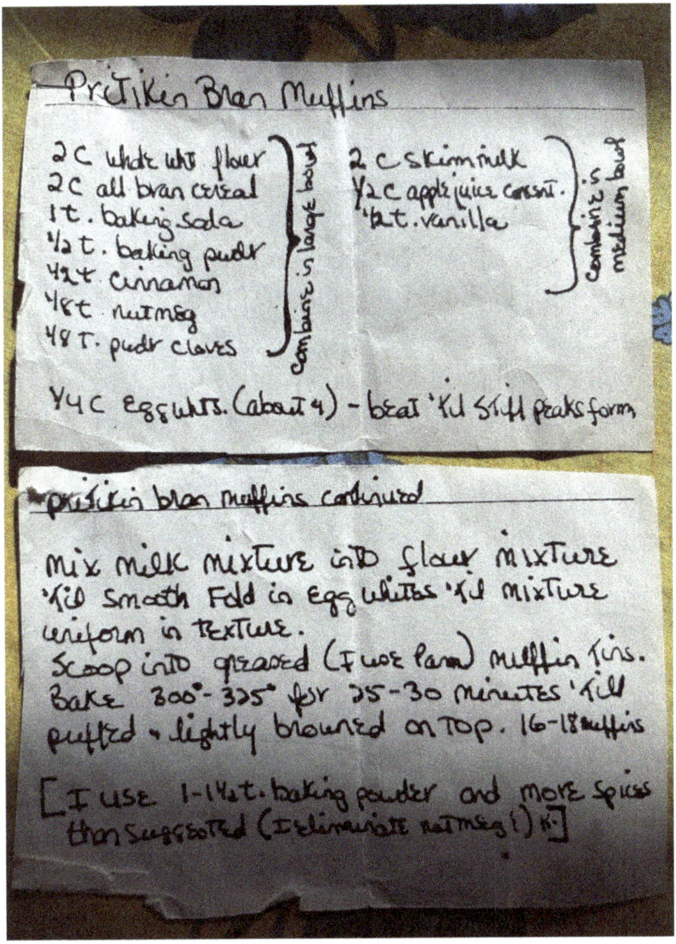

Pritikin Bran Muffins

2 C white wht flour ⎫
2 C all bran cereal ⎪
1 t. baking soda ⎪
½ t. baking powder ⎬ Combine in large bowl
½ t cinnamon ⎪
¼ t. nutmeg ⎪
¼ T. pwdr cloves ⎭

2 c skim milk ⎫
½ C apple juice consnt. ⎬ Combine in medium bowl
1 t. vanilla ⎭

¾ C egg whts. (about 4) – beat 'til stiff peaks form

_____

Pritikin bran muffins continued

Mix milk mixture into flour mixture 'til smooth. Fold in egg whites 'til mixture uniform in texture.
Scoop into greased (I use Pam) muffin tins.
Bake 300°–325° for 25–30 minutes 'till puffed & lightly browned on top. 16–18 muffins

[I use 1–1½ t. baking powder and more spices than suggested (I eliminate nutmeg!) ½"]

English Popovers

INGREDIENTS

Wet

1 cup milk
3 eggs
1 tbsp salad oil

Dry

1 cup flour
½ tsp salt

DIRECTIONS

Blend wet ingredients in a blender on high until well
mixed, then add the dry ingredients and beat until
smooth.
Pour into a well-greased muffin pans ½ full.
Bake 475 deg. 15 minutes, then lower the temperature to
350 deg for 25-30 minutes longer.
A few minutes prior to removing from the oven, prick
them with a fork.

NOTES

This is a form of Yorkshire pudding. When I was a child,
my mother and grandmother always said to add fat to the
pan and heat in the oven until almost smoking before
pouring in the batter.

Contributed by Sheila Lowe

Popovers

makes 6-8

1 C milk
3 eggs
1 T salad oil
½ t s.
1 C flour

} blender @ high til s mixed
add flour til smooth

Pour into well-greased muffin pans
½ full. Bake 475° 15 mins; 350° 25-30 mins longer.
A few minutes prior to rem. from oven prick w. fork.

21

INGREDIENTS

Wet

18 little Rhodes rolls (frozen) in 'Pammed' bundt pan.

1 stick butter

Dry

½ box butterscotch pudding (not instant)
½ cup walnuts
½ cup sugar

½ cup brown sugar

DIRECTIONS

Mix together dry ingredients. Spread on rolls.
Melt butter, mix with brown sugar.
Drizzle on rolls.
Bake…? (Ed. Note: suggest 25-35 minutes at 350 degrees)

NOTES

Contributed by Peg Brantley

Sticky Buns

18 little Rhodes rolls (frozen)
in pammed bundt pan

Mix together
  1/2 box Butterscotch
       pudding (NOT instant)
  1/2 c Walnuts
  1/2 c Sugar

Spread on rolls.
Melt 1 stick butter &
1/2 c brown sugar.
Drizzle on rolls.
plum fril over pan
hot rise overnite

350°
5 min

Chocolate Flan Cake

CAKE INGREDIENTS

Cooking spray
Mrs. Richardson's Smuckers Caramel Topping
1 cup water (or ½ milk)
5 large eggs
½ cup **Crisco** pure vegetable oil (others may leave an aftertaste)
1Devils food cake mix (15.25 oz)

FLAN

1 can Eagle Brand condensed milk (14 oz)
1 can Pet evaporated milk (12 oz)
5 large eggs (room temp)
8 oz cream cheese, softened
1 tsp vanilla extract
1 tsp almond extract

DIRECTIONS

Coat 12 cup fluted tube pan with non-stick cooking spray. Place a piece of rolled-up foil in the tube to prevent spillage. Pour caramel topping into prepared pan.

Beat cake mix, water/milk, 3 eggs and oil until well combined; pour evenly over caramel topping.

Combine condensed milk, evaporated milk, 4 eggs, cream cheese, vanilla in a blender. Process until smooth. Slowly pour over cake batter. The cake will rise while baking, and milk mixture will sink to the bottom.

Coat a piece of foil with nonstick spray, cover pan tightly with foil, coated side down. Place pan in a large roasting pan and pour hot water in pan to a depth of 2 inches.

Preheat oven to 350 and bake 2 hours until toothpick inserted in center comes out with a few moist crumbs.

Place cake on cooling rack for 15 minutes, then remove foil and invert on serving plate. Cool 1 hour at room temp, chill 4 hours or overnight. *Enjoy the compliments!*

Contributed by Linda Larson

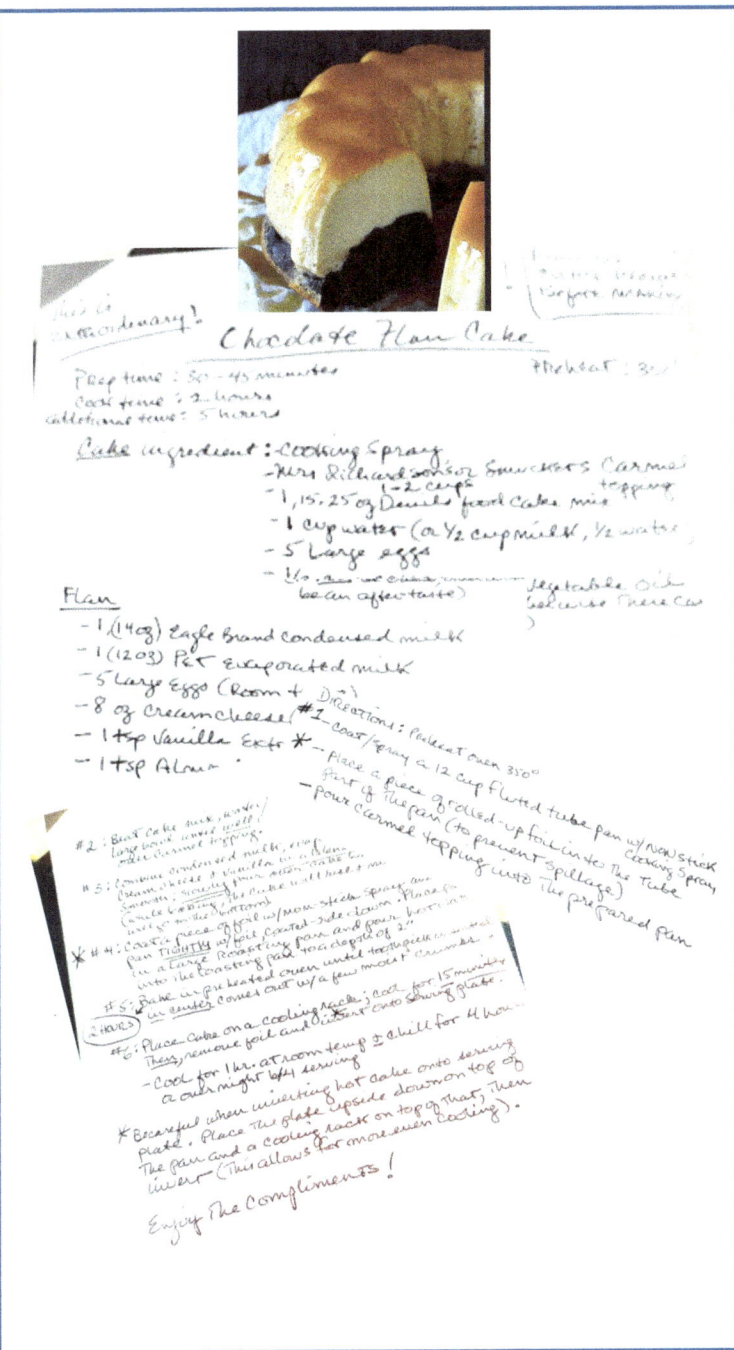

This is extraordinary!

Chocolate Flan Cake

Prep time: 30 - 45 minutes
Cook time: 2 hours
additional time: 5 hours

*Preheat: 350°

<u>Cake ingredients:</u> Cooking Spray
- Mrs Richardson's 8 oz Sundaes Carmel topping
- 1, 15.25 oz Devil's Food Cake mix 1-2 cups
- 1 cup water (or ½ cup milk, ½ water)
- 5 Large eggs
- ⅓ ~~cup oil~~ vegetable oil (releases there cus) (can be an after taste)

<u>Flan</u>
- 1 (14 oz) Eagle Brand condensed milk
- 1 (12 oz) PET Evaporated milk
- 5 Large Eggs (Room + Dir'ns)
- 8 oz cream cheese
- 1 tsp Vanilla Extr *
- 1 tsp Almond

<u>Directions:</u>
#1 - Preheat oven 350°
- coat/spray a 12 cup fluted tube pan w/ non-stick
- Place a piece of rolled-up foil into the tube cooking spray
part of the pan (to prevent spillage)
- Pour carmel topping into the prepared pan

#2: Beat Cake mix, water, [over] large bowl mixed well,
add carmel topping

#3: Combine condensed milk, evaporated
milk, cream cheese + vanilla til blend.
Smooth, slowly pour over cake. This
will go to the bottom
~~Candle~~ coating the cake will melt in

#4: Cover pan w/ foil coated-side down. Place a
pan tightly w/ foil coated-side down. Place in
a large Roasting pan and pour boiling water
into the roasting pan to a depth of 2"

#5: Bake in preheated oven until toothpick in
center comes out w/ a few moist crumbs.
(2 hours)

#6: Place Cake on a cooling rack; cool for 15 min.
Then remove foil and invert onto serving plate.
- Cool for 1 hr. at room temp + chill for 4 hours
or overnight before serving

* Be careful when inverting hot cake onto serving
plate. Place the plate upside down on top of
the pan and a cooling rack on top of that, then
invert (This allows for more even cooling).

Enjoy the Compliments!

Black Walnut Cake

INGREDIENTS

Wet

1 cup Wesson oil
2 eggs
1 cup buttermilk

Dry

2 cups self-rising flour
1 ½ cup sugar
1 cup black walnuts
1 tsp baking powder
1 tsp cinnamon
1 tsp nutmeg

DIRECTIONS

Beat eggs and sugar, buttermilk together.
Mix dry ingredients together and mix with wet ingredients.
Bake in a large pan at 300 degrees for one hour.

Sauce

1 ½ cup sugar, 1 stick margarine, 1 cup buttermilk, 1 tsp.
Baking soda, 1 tsp vanilla.
Bring to a boil, pour over cake while hot.

NOTES

Contributed by Bessie Porter via Helene Robinson

BESSIE PORTER
PICKENS, SC

Black Walnut Butter Milk Cake

1½ Cup sugar   1 C Wesson Oil

2 eggs

   Mix Together   1 tsp Cinnamon

2 C. Self rising flour | 1 tsp nutmeg

1 C. Butter milk   1 cup Black Walnut

1 tsp soda

   Mix dry ingredients together then Mix
with sugar and egg mixture. Bake in a
large pan at 300 degrees for 1 hour

Sauce:

1½ C sugar   1 tsp. soda

1 stick margarine   1 tsp Vanilla

1 Cup Butter milk

   Bring To a boil, pour over cake while hot

Mike Roy's Strawberry Cake

INGREDIENTS

Wet

¾ cup frozen strawberries
4 eggs
½ cup vegetable oil

Dry

1 box white cake mix
1 box (3 oz) strawberry jello

DIRECTIONS

Drain the berries (reserve juice).
Combine cake mix, jello, eggs. Beat two minutes on low.
Add oil, juice, beat two more minutes to make a thin batter.
Fold in the berries.
Pour into greased and floured 9 x 13 pan.
Bake thirty-five minutes at 350 degrees.
Frost with whipped cream and fresh strawberries.

NOTES

Back in the 1970s, Chef Mike Roy wrote cookbooks and share recipes on the radio. I've included several of them in this book.

Contributed by Sheila Lowe

Mike Kay's STRAWBERRY cake

Strawberries

3/4 C strawbs (Frozen)

White Cake mix
1 · 3z Strawb. Jello
4 eggs
1/2 C oil

Frost w.
whipped
cream

Drain berries.
Combine mix, Jello, eggs. beat 2 mins on Low
add oil, Juice, beat 2 mins. (Thin batter) more
Fold in Berries. Pour in prep. 9x13 pan
350° 35 mins

31

Przekładaniec Ciasto

Polish Honey Cake with currants (3 cakes)

INGREDIENTS

Dough

4 cups flour
2 cup granulated sugar
1/3 cup + 1 Tbsp butter
2 eggs
1 level tsp baking soda
2 Tbsp honey
3 Tbsp sour cream

Cream filling

2 cups milk
6 tablespoons semolina
1/8 cup butter (just under)
Currant jam with no added sugar or other gelling agents. Currants have their own specific natural sour taste, which will give character and balance the flavor of the cake.

DIRECTIONS

Dough: Mix all the ingredients, add melted butter (slightly warm). Knead dough by hand and divide into 3 equal parts. Roll out each into a thin cake and shape it to fit the baking tray. Bake the sheets individually in the oven at 350 for 10 minutes each until golden brown. Cool before filling.

Filling: Cream ¾ cup of butter. Add the cooled semolina to the creamed butter one spoonful at a time and stir. After mixing, the butter and semolina will form a white, fluffy mixture. Spread the semolina mixture and currant jam on the three baked cakes in the following order: Semolina mixture on the first cake, cover with the second cake, spread the currant jam on the second cake and cover the whole thing with the third cake.

Bon appétit!

Contributed by Aleksandra Esveld-Cieśla via Rafal Cieśla

Placek miodowy z pęcakiem (3 placki)

Składniki

Ciasto:
- 1½ kg mąki
- 20 dg cukru pudru
- 7 dg masła
- 2 jajka
- 1 płaska łyżeczka sody
- 2 łyżki stołowe miodu
- 3 łyżki kwaśnej śmietany

Krem (masa):
- 2 szklanki mleka
- 6 łyżek kaszy manny (pęcak)
- 18 dg masła
- olzem pęcakowy 100% (najlepiej 100%, bo dodatkowe cukry czy inngd sok będzie pęcaka ma swój specyficzny naturalny kwaskowaty smak, który nada charakteru i zbalansuje smak ciasta)

Wykonanie ciasta

Wymieszać wszystkie składniki, masło dodajemy rozpuszczone (lekko ciepłe) i zagnieść ciasto (wyrobić gęste) i podzielić na 2 równe części. Każdą część rozwałkować na cienki placek i uformować kształt dopasowany do blytfanki. Placki piec w piekarniku pojedynczo na złoto w temperaturze 170°C przez około 10 min każdy. Przed nałożeniem masy placki muszą być ostudzone.

Wykonanie kremu (masy)

Pęcak wrzucamy na wrzące gotowane mleko, mieszamy przez 3 min. Do gorącego pęcaku wsypać 15 dg cukru i wymieszać. Odstawić do ostudzenia, wystygnięcia. Utrzeć 18 dg masła (w maselnice drewniana pałką lub widamy dodajemy szybciej). Do utartego masła dodawać po łyżce ostudzony pęcak i mieszać. Masło razem z pęcakiem po wymieszaniu utworzy biała puszysta masę. Upieczone 3 placki należy przełożyć masą pęcakową i dziewiku pęcakowym w następującej kolejności: na pierwszy placek nakładamy masę pęcakową, następnie przykrywamy ją drugim plackiem na który nakładamy dżem pożiarkowy, a trzecim plackiem przykrywamy całość. Smacznego!

Tort Jabłkowy Ciasto

Polish Apple Cake

INGREDIENTS

Cake

2 ¾ cups flour
1 cup butter
¾ cup sugar
A pinch of salt
1 egg

Filling

6-8 medium apples (firm apples (e.g. Golden Delicious, Prince), include 1 Grey Rennet apple because it is sour)
1 packet vanilla sugar
1 heaping Tbsp raisins
¾ cup cranberries (or substitute raisins for cranberries)
1 egg yolk

DIRECTIONS

Mix all the ingredients and knead the dough, divide into two parts. Line the bottom of a round cake pan with one part. Grease sides of the cake pan with butter and sprinkle with a little semolina. Roll out the second part and cut it into strips to form a so-called checkerboard pattern on top of the apple filling.

Filling

Peel the apples, cut into quarters and slice, then mix in a bowl with the other ingredients, i.e. raisins, cranberries and vanilla sugar. After mixing, pour the apples into a roasting pan lined with dough and arrange strips of dough in a lattice pattern on top of the apples. Then brush the lattice strips with egg yolk to give them a better flavor and golden color. Bake for about an hour at at 390 degrees.   *Bon appétit!*

Contributed by Anna Esveld via Rafal Cieśla

Tort jabłkowy

ciasto:

350 gram mąki
210 gram masła
150 gram cukru
troszkę soli
1 jajko

nadzienie:

6-8 średnich jabłek twardych
nie rozpadających się w pieczeniu
(np. Jonagold, Champion i
jedna szara reneta.)
1 paczka cukru waniliowego
80 gram rodzynek
20 gram suszonej żurawiny
(można zamiast żurawiny dać 20g rodzynek)
1 żółtko.

Przygotowanie ciasta.

Wymieszać wszystkie składniki i zagnieść ciasto.
Następnie podzielić na dwie części. Jedną częścią
wyłożyć spód okrągłej brytfanki (24cm). Brytfankę
smaruję po bokach masłem i obsypuję troszeczkę
np. kaszą manną. Drugą część ciasta rozwałkowuję
i wycinam paski, które ułożę w kratkę na nadzieniu
z jabłek.

Przygotowanie nadzienia

Jabłka obieram ze skórek, przekrawam na ćwiartki i kroję
w plasterki, następnie mieszam je w misce z pozostałymi
składnikami tj. rodzynkami, żurawiny i cukrem waniliowym.
Następnie wysypuję te jabłka na wyłożoną ciastem brytfankę
i układam na jabłkach paski z ciasta w kratkę, a następnie
Te paski smaruję żółtkiem jajka dla lepszego smaku i koloru.
Ciasto wkładam do rozgrzanego piekarnika i piec w 200° przez godzinę.
Smacznego!

Crushed Pineapple Cake

INGREDIENTS

Wet

1 large can crushed
pineapple with juice
2 eggs

Dry

2 cups flour
2 cups sugar
2 tsp soda
8 oz chopped nuts

DIRECTIONS

Mix everything well in one bowl, pour in 9 x 12 pan.
(Ed. Note: cooking directions are missing. My guess, bake
for 25 - 40 minutes at 350).

NOTES

Contributed by Ruth Holmes

Crushed Pineapple Cake

2 cups flour
2 cups sugar
2 tsp. soda
1 large can crushed pineapple (juice too)
2 eggs
8 oz. chopped nuts

Mix everything well in one bowl put in 9x12 pan

Banana Split Cake

INGREDIENTS

Wet
4 Tbsp diet margarine
1 pkg low cal vanilla pudding
2 medium bananas
2 cups well-drained pineapple
1 cup Cool Whip

Dry
16 graham cracker squares
2 Tbsp + 2 tsp Hershey's syrup

DIRECTIONS

Crush graham crackers, mix with margarine and press into 8" or 9" pan.
Prepare the pudding according to package directions, spread on crumbs.
Slice bananas on pudding. Spread pineapple on top of bananas. Spread Cool Whip on top of pineapple.
Drizzle chocolate syrup on top.
Cut into 8 servings.

NOTES

Contributed by Peg Brantley

Banana Split Cake - Serves 8   WW

16 graham cracker squares (made into crumbs)
4 Tbsp. diet margarine

Mix crumbs & margarine; press into 8" or 9" pan.

1 pkg. low calorie vanilla pudding (make
according to pkg directions & chill). Spread
on crumbs.

2 medium bananas, sliced on top of pudding

2 c. well drained pineapple spread on
top of bananas.

1 c. Cool Whip spread on top of pineapple.

2 T + 2 t Hershey's syrup,
drizzled on top.

Cut into 8 Servings. Each:

   1 B   1 M   3/4 FA

   1 FR   45 C

Mandarin Mousse Cheesecake

INGREDIENTS

Wet

3 pkg orange jello
1 cup boiling water
1 can evaporated milk
2/3 cup melted margarine
2 cans mandarin oranges

Dry

2 cups graham crumbs
¼ cup sugar
2 Tbsp cornstarch
½ cup sugar

DIRECTIONS

Dissolve two packages of jello in 1 cup boiling water.
Cool to room temperature.

Chill evaporated milk in freezer one hour.

Crust: combine graham crumbs, ¼ cup sugar, and
margarine, and press evenly into 13 x 9 pan.

Whip chilled evaporated milk until soft peaks form. Mix
in cooled jello. Pour over crust and refrigerate two hours.

Drain mandarin oranges (save liquid), arrange mandarin
sections on mousse layer.

Glaze: in a saucepan, add water to mandarin juice to
make 1 cup. Combine with ½ cup sugar and cornstarch,
then cook until thick. Add one package orange jello, stir
to completely dissolve. Carefully spoon over orange
sections.

Keep refrigerated until serving.

Contributed by Edda Manley

Mandarin Mousse Cheesecake
13 × 9 pan

Dissolve 2 packages orange jello in
1 c. boiling water. Cool to room
temperature.
Chill one can evaporated milk in
freezer 1 hour.

Crust: 2 c. graham crumbs
       1/4 c. sugar
       2/3 c. melted margarine
Press evenly into 13 × 9 pan.
Whip chilled evaporated milk
until soft peaks form.
Mix cooled jello into stiff evaporated
milk. Pour over graham crust.
Refrigerate 2 hours.
Drain 2 cans mandarin
oranges (save liquid to make glaze.
Arrange oranges on mousse layer.
Glaze: Use mandarin juice and
      add water to make 1 cup
      in saucepan combine with
      2 tbsp. cornstarch
      1/2 c sugar and cook until
      thick. Add one package
      orange jello, stir to dissolve
      completely. Carefully spoon over
      orange sections
Keep refrigerated until serving time

Paula's Poppyseed Cake

INGREDIENTS

Wet

1 ½ cups cooking oil
1 cup milk
4 eggs
1 tsp vanilla

Dry

3 cups flour
2 cups sugar
1 tsp. salt
2 oz poppy seed
½ cup chopped nuts

DIRECTIONS

Mix dry ingredients in bowl. Add remaining ingredients (except nuts) and beat 5 minutes at high speed. Stir in nuts.

Pour into greased and floured tube pan or two loaf pans or muffin cups.

Bake at 350 deg. for one hour (+/-)

NOTES

Contributed by Paula Coats via Peg Brantley

Recipe from: _Paula Coats_

Date:

Poppy Seed Cake

3 cups flour; 1 tsp. salt;
2 oz. poppy seed; 4 eggs;
1½ cups oil; 2 cups
sugar; 1 tsp. soda; 1 tsp.
vanilla; 1 cup milk; ½
cup chopped nuts.

Put dry ingredients in bowl
add remainder and beat
5 minutes at high speed.
Add nuts and stir.

Pour into greased; floured
tube* pan. Bake @ 350°
for 1 hr (+/-)

* Can use loaf pans or
muffin cups

Mary's Poppyseed Cake

INGREDIENTS

Wet

4 eggs
1 cup water
½ cup oil

Dry

1 stick butter
1 lg pkg vanilla pudding
¼ cup poppy seeds

DIRECTIONS

Beat all, pour into greased/floured bundt pan and bake 45-55 minutes at 350 degrees.

NOTES

Contributed by Mary Gabriels (The Netherlands)

POPPY SEED CAKE

1 PKG. BUTTER CAKE MIX -YELLOW
(BETTY CROCKER W/ PUDDING)

4 EGGS

Jacqui's Poppyseed Cake

INGREDIENTS

Wet

3 eggs, beaten
½ cup oil
1 cup plain yogurt

Dry

1 ½ cups sugar
4 Tbsp poppy seeds
1 cup coconut
1 cup self-raising flour

DIRECTIONS

Combine beaten eggs with sugar until light and fluffy. Add remaining ingredients. Beat together, pour into buttered pan and bake 40-45 minutes at 350 degrees.

Frosting
In double boiler cook 1.25 cups white chocolate, 8 Tbsp confectioner's sugar, 6 Tbsp milk. Remove from stove and add 3 tsp butter, 1 tsp vanilla, and pour over cake.

NOTES

Contributed by Terry Elmaleh (South Africa)

Poppy Seed Cake

Beat 3 eggs
Add 1½ cups sugar until light & fluffy
½ cup oil
50 grams poppy seed
100 grams coconut
1 cup self raising flour (+ 2 tsp)
250 ml of plain yoghurt (or sp)
Beat all together, pour into buttered dish & bake 180° 40-45min
Cook in double boiler - 900 grams white chocolate,
8 Tables. Icing Sugar, 6 Tables Milk. Take off stove
& add 3 tbs butter & 1 tbs vanilla & pour over cake

Armenian Cake

INGREDIENTS

Wet

½ cup butter
1 cup sour cream

Dry

2 cups brown sugar
2 cups flour
1 tsp baking soda
Cinnamon
Nutmeg
Allspice
Chopped nuts

DIRECTIONS

Cut sugar and flour with butter. Remove half and pat into bottom of 8" baking pan.
To remaining half add spices, sour cream, baking soda.
Pour over pan, sprinkle with chopped nuts.
Bake 40 minutes at 350 degrees.

NOTES

Contributed by Carla Winter

Armenian Cake   8" pan   350°

2 cup Brown sugar ⎫ cut w/ fork, remove half
2 cup Flour   ⎬ and pat into bottom of
½ cup Butter   ⎭ pan

To remaining half add:
cinamon, nutmeg, allspice
1 cup SOUR CREAM
1 Tsp SODA
pour over pan, sprinkle CHOPPED NUTS
40 min. 350°

Ruthie's Pumpkin Bars

INGREDIENTS

Wet

¾ cup butter
4 eggs
1 can (2 cups) pumpkin

Dry

2 cups sugar
2 cups flour
2 tsp baking powder
½ - 1 tsp cinnamon
1 tsp baking soda
¾ cup nuts

DIRECTIONS

Mix butter, sugar, eggs, pumpkin until fluffy.
Add dry ingredients.
Pour into greased and floured 11 x 15 cookie sheet.
Frost with powdered sugar

NOTES

Contributed by Monique Brockley Drinkman

Ruthie Pumpkin Bars   350°

3/4 c butter   Mix til fluffy
2 c sugar
4 eggs
1 15 z can (2c) pumpkin
add
2 c flour
2 tsp BP.
1/2 - 1 tsp cinnamon
1 tsp soda
3/4 c nuts.

11"X15"X1" greased & floured cookie
sheet
    Frost with Powdered Sugar

Lauren's Luscious Pumpkin Cake

INGREDIENTS

Wet

Almost 1 can (32 oz) pumpkin (leave 1 inch in can)
1 cup vegetable oil
4 eggs (room temperature)

Dry

1 cups flour
2 tsp baking powder
2 tsp cinnamon
1 tsp cloves
1 tsp ginger
¼ tsp nutmeg

DIRECTIONS

Mix eggs, sugar, then pumpkin and oil. Add dry ingredients.
Bake for 50 minutes to one hour at 325 degrees.
Frost with cream cheese frosting (add rum flavoring)

NOTES

Contributed by Lauren Mooney Bear

4 egg
room temp.

Pumpkin Cake

2 cups flour
2 teasp bk. powl.
2 T ~~baking soda~~ ⎫ cinnamon
1 T clover ⎬ combine
1 T ginger ⎭
1/4 T nutmeg.

almost 1 can pumpkin (leave 1 in. in can)
32 oz
2 C sugar
1 cup oil
4 eggs

mix eggs, sugar & then pumpkin
& oil. Then dry ingredients
325° - 50 min to 1 hr.

Frost cream cheese frosting
Rum flavor

Vasilopita

INGREDIENTS

Wet

4 large eggs, separated
Zest of 1 orange
½ cup unsalted butter
softened at room temp,
plus more to grease the
pan.
1 cup freshly squeezed
orange juice
2 Tbsp brandy (optional)
1 tsp vanilla extract

Dry

2 ¾ cups all-purpose
flour
1 tsp baking powder
¼ teaspoon baking
soda
¼ teaspoon salt
1 cup granulated sugar
Foil-wrapped coin

DIRECTIONS

Separate the eggs. Beat the whites until stiff peaks form.
In another bowl, combine dry ingredients. Set aside. In a
large bowl, combine sugar and orange zest. Beat with
butter until light and creamy. Beat in egg yolks one at a
time. Slowly beat in orange juice, brandy, vanilla. Fold in
1/3 egg whites, followed by 1/3 of the flour mixture.
Continue with 1/3 egg whites, 1/3 flour, then remaining
egg whites and remaining flour, just until no streaks
remain. Take care not to deflate the egg whites. Stir a foil-
wrapped coin into the batter, pour all into prepared pan.

Bake in the preheated oven until the edges are golden
brown and a toothpick inserted in the center comes out
clean, 35-40 minutes. Do not open the oven door until
the cake is nearly done.

Allow to cool to room temperature before decorating and
dusting with a layer of powdered sugar.

Whoever gets the coin wins a year of great good luck!

Contributed by Fiona Manning

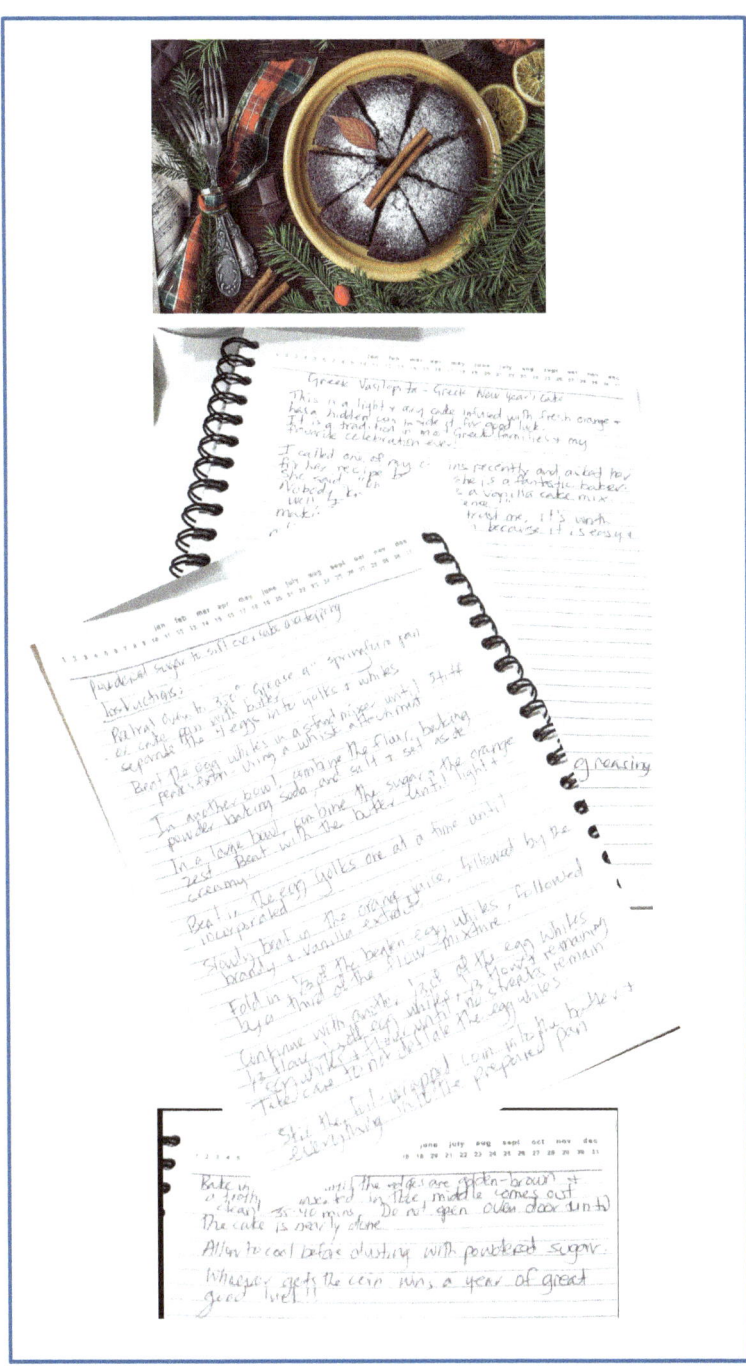

Greek Vasilopita - Greek New Year's Cake

This is a light + airy cake infused with fresh orange + ___ A hidden coin inside it for good luck. Having a celebration are Greek families is my ___

I called one of my cousins recently and asked her for her recipe ___ she is a fantastic baker. Nobody knows ___ is a vanilla cake mix ___ ___ make ___ trust me, it's worth ___ ___ because it's easy ___

Powdered sugar to sift over cake at keeping

Instructions:
Preheat oven to 350°. Grease a 9" springform pan
Separate the 7 eggs into yolks + whites ___ separate bowls.
Beat the egg whites in a stand mixer until stiff peaks form using a whisk attachment
In another bowl, combine the flour, baking powder, baking soda and salt + set aside
In a large bowl, combine the sugar + the orange zest. Beat with the butter until light + creamy
Beat in the egg yolks one at a time until incorporated
Slowly beat in the orange juice, followed by the brandy + vanilla extract
Fold in 1/3 of the beaten egg whites by a third of the flour mixture
Continue with another third of the egg whites + flour until no streaks remain ___ being careful not to deflate the egg whites
Take care to not deflate the egg whites
Scrape the batter into the prepared pan
Stir the foil-wrapped coin into batter ___

greasing

Bake in ___ until the edges are golden-brown + a toothpick inserted in the middle comes out clean ___ 35-40 mins. Do not open oven door until the cake is nearly done

Allow to cool before dusting with powdered sugar.

Whoever gets the coin wins a year of great good luck!!

Fruitcake

INGREDIENTS

Wet

1 ½ cup water
¼ cup butter
2 eggs, beaten

1 lb washed raisins
1 lb glazed fruit

Dry

2 ½ cups flour
1 ½ cup sugar
1 tsp baking powder
1 tsp baking soda
½ tsp allspice
½ tsp salt
1 tsp cinnamon
½ cup nuts

DIRECTIONS

A few days before making, pour brandy over fruit.
Boil together water, raisins, sugar, butter for five minutes, and cool.
Sift dry ingredients together.
Add eggs to dry ingredients and add to boiled mixture.
Bake two hours at 250 degrees.

NOTES

My mother, Paula Jean, had an annual fruitcake tradition and collected old coffee tins to bake the cakes in. Without the glazed fruit, the cake was delicious. Yuck to the glazed fruit. Yay to extra brandy pre-soaking.

Contributed by Carla Winter (in her own handwriting)

FRUITCAKE   250° OVEN
pan Tin of H2O
2 hrs.

1. 1½ C. H2O
2. 1 lb washed raisin
3. 1½ cu. sugar
4. ¼ cu. Butter
5. 2 beaten eggs
6. 2½ cu. flour
7. 1 Tsp Bak pw/
8. 1 Tsp Soda.
9. ½ Tsp Allspice
10. ½ Tsp Salt

11. 1 Tsp Cina.
12. ½ Tsp Clove
13. 1 lb glazed fru.
14. ½ cu. nuts

→ Boil together 5 min.
Sift dry incrediants
cool Boiled stuff a little
Mix eggs to Dry & a boil –
– few days before Take fruit
& xtra. Pour Brandy over

Bud's Blueberry Cake

INGREDIENTS

Wet

1 egg
½ cup milk
3 Tbsp shortening
1 tsp vanilla extract

1 ½ cups blueberries

Dry

1 cup sugar
1 ½ cups sifted flour
1 ½ tsp baking powder

DIRECTIONS

Cream together the sugar and shortening.
Combine egg, milk, flour, baking powder, vanilla.
Fold in blueberries.
(Ed note: Combine wet and dry ingredients?)
Sprinkle mixture of cinnamon sugar on top of batter before baking.
Bake 35 minutes at 350 degrees.

NOTES

Contributed by Ruth Holmes

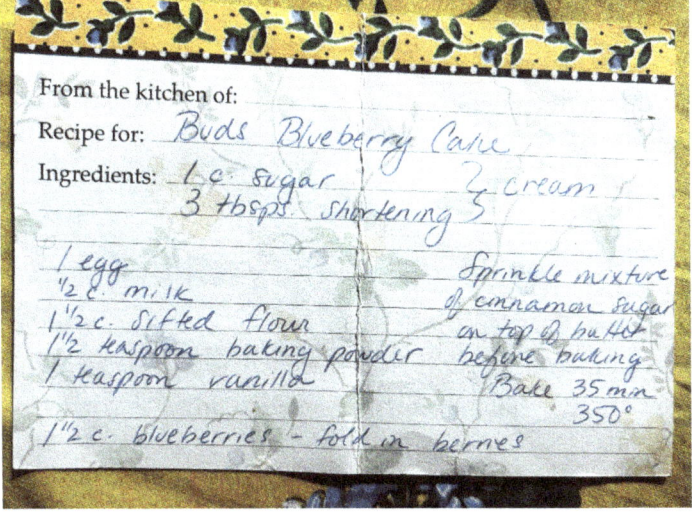

From the kitchen of:

Recipe for: Buds Blueberry Cake

Ingredients: 1 c. sugar   2 cream
3 tbsps. Shortening   5

1 egg   Sprinkle mixture
1/2 c. milk   of cinnamon sugar
1 1/2 c. sifted flour   on top of butter
1 1/2 teaspoon baking powder   before baking
1 teaspoon vanilla   Bake 35 min
                                  350°
1 1/2 c. blueberries - fold in berries

59

Harvey Wallbanger Cake

INGREDIENTS

Wet

½ cup oil
4 eggs
¼ cup vodka
¼ cup Galliano
¾ cup orange juice

Dry

1 pkg white cake mix
1 pkg instant vanilla pudding

DIRECTIONS

Beat together all ingredients. Pour into greased and floured bundt cake pan. Bake for 50 minutes at 350 degrees. Sprinkle with sugar and grated lemon rind.

NOTES

Another Chef Mike Roy recipe for those who like a little zing in their dessert. Most of the alcohol cooks off in the oven, but you might want a designated driver if you have seconds.

Contributed by Sheila Lowe

Mike Roy's   Harvey Wallbanger Cake

1 pk white cake mix
1 pk Instant Van. pud.
½ C oil
4 eggs
¼ C Vodka
¼ C galliano
¾ C O.J.

Beat 4 mins
Pour into prep. pans 350° 50 mins
Sprinkle w. sugar – grated lem. rind

Gluten Free Chocolate Cake

INGREDIENTS

Wet

1 cups milk (dairy or non)
3 eggs
½ cup vegetable oil
2 tsp vanilla
1 cup boiling water

Dry

1 ¾ cup of GF flour*
2 cups sugar
¾ cup cocoa
2 tsp baking powder
1 ½ tsp baking soda
1 tsp salt
1 tsp xanthan gum

DIRECTIONS

In a large mixing bowl, combine eggs, oil, vanilla, milk and sugar. Blend well.

In a separate bowl, combine the rest of the dry ingredients. Add the dry ingredients to the wet in small quantities, mixing in between. Mix well.

Add the boiling water, mix for only 30 seconds. Batter will be thin. Pour into 9 x 13 pan.

Bake for 30-35 minutes at 350 degrees.

NOTES

King Arthur cup for cup measure has Xanthan gum in it.

Contributed by Pat Carter

Gluten Free Chocolate Cake

Ingredients:
* 1¾ cup of GF flour + 2 cups of sugar
3/4 cup cocoa
2 Tsp baking powder
1 1/2 Tsp baking soda
1 Tsp salt
1 Tsp XNTHAN GUM
3 eggs
1 cup milk (dairy or non)
1/2 cup vegetable oil
2 Tsp vanilla
1 cup boiling water

Directions:
In a large mixing bowl, combine eggs, oil
vanilla, milk and sugar. Blend well.
In a separate bowl, the rest of the dry
ingredients. Add the dry ingredients to
the wet in small quantities, mixing in
between. Mix well.
Add the boiling water, mix for only 30 secs.
Batter will be thin.
Pour into 9x13 inch pan
Bake at 350° for 30-35 minutes.

* King Arthur cup for cup measure has
XNTHAN GUM in it.

Chocolate Gateau

INGREDIENTS

Wet

1 ½ cups chocolate
½ cup butter
4 eggs, separated

Dry

1 ¼ cups powdered sugar
2 Tbsp flour

DIRECTIONS

Melt chocolate in a saucepan.
Melt butter. Mix together.

In a bowl mix together the powdered sugar, flour, 4 egg yolks.
Beat 4 egg whites until stiff. Fold all together and pour into a cake pan.
Bake for 25 minutes at 350 degrees

(Ed. Note: gateau is often layered with whipped cream or mousse with fruit accents)

NOTES

I love good food, except I always prefer if someone else cooks it for me.

Contributed by Laurence Baudot (France)

Gâteau au chocolat

- Faire fondre dans une casserole
  250 gr de chocolat
- Faire fondre 120 gr de beurre
- Dans un récipient mélangez :

  - 150 gr de sucre en poudre
  - 2 grandes cuillères de farine

- Ajoutez 4 jaunes d'œuf
- Montez 4 blancs d'œuf en neige

- Mélangez.

- Faire cuire pendant 25 minutes

Aunt Tillie's Chocolate Cake

INGREDIENTS

Wet

1 cup sour cream
4 large eggs
½ cup vegetable oil
½ cup warm water
¼ cup Kahlua

Dry

18 ½ oz pkg chocolate cake with pudding in the mix.
4 oz pkg instant chocolate pudding
12 oz semi-sweet chocolate chips
Powdered sugar
Zest of an orange

DIRECTIONS

Preheat oven to 350 deg.
Blend all ingredients (chips last)
Pour into greased and flour bundt pan.
Bake 50-60 minutes at 350 degrees
After cooling, finish with powdered sugar and orange zest.

NOTES

Happy baking!

Contributed by Katrina Garvey

Aunt Tillie's Chocolate Cake:

<u>Ingredients</u> :
- 18½ oz pkg chocolate cake, with pudding in the mix
- 1 c sour cream
- 4 large eggs.
- ½ c. vegetable oil
- 4oz pkg instant chocolate pudding
- ½ c. warm water
- ¼ c. Kaluha
- 12oz semi-sweet chocolate chips
- Powdered sugar
- zested orange peel.

<u>Directions</u>:
1. Preheat oven to 350°
2. Blend all ingredients (choc chips go in last).
3. Put in a greased + floured bundt pan.
4. Bake 50-60 min.
5. After cooling, finish with powdered sugar and orange zest.

Happy Baking! _K

INGREDIENTS

Wet

2 cups cold water
Corn oil (how much???)
2 Tbsp white vinegar

Dry

3 cups flour
2 cups sugar
2/3 cup unsweetened cocoa
1 tsp salt

DIRECTIONS

Sift together dry ingredients.
In a separate bowl, mix together wet ingredients. Pour through strainer into a bowl. Mix again, and pour into pan.
Tap the edge of the pan against the counter to release air bubbles.
Bake for 25-30 minutes at 350 degrees.

NOTES

Contributed by Ruth Holmes

Chocolate Cake

- 3 cups flour
- 2/3 cup unsweetened cocoa
- 2 tsp baking soda
- 2 cups sugar
- 1 tsp salt

- 2 cups cold water
- 1/2 cup + 2 Tb corn oil
- 2 Tb white vinegar

Mix together dry ingredients. Sift. In separate bowl, mix together wet ingredients. Pour through strainer into a bowl. Mix again, and pour into pan. Tap the edge of the pan against the counter to release air bubbles. Bake at 350° for 25 to 30 min.

Cookies

Franks Famous Chocolate Chip Cookies

INGREDIENTS

Wet

1 cup real butter, salted
1 cup granulated sugar
1 cup brown sugar
2 eggs
1 tsp vanilla

Dry

2 cups all-purpose flour
1 tsp baking soda
1 tsp baking powder
1 tsp salt

2 cups rolled oats (not instant)

1 pkg chocolate chips

DIRECTIONS

Mix the wet ingredients together well
Mix together the dry ingredients
Blend all together.
Add rolled oats and chocolate chips
Drop spoonfuls onto parchment paper
Bake for approximately 15 minutes at 350 degrees
Enjoy!

NOTES

I once owned Frank's Famous Kitchen and Bakery in Southern California. One customer wrote about this cookie: *"It's amazing! The best I ever tasted...You will have no regrets and will want more."*

Contributed by Frank Dutro

Frank's Famous
Chocolate Chip Cookies

The Wet Stuff

1 Cup real butter, Salted
1 Cup Sugar
1 Cup Brown sugar
2 Eggs
1 TSP Vanilla
        mix well together

Dry Stuff
2 Cups All Purpose Flour
1 TSP Baking Soda
1 TSP Baking Powder
1 TSP Salt
        mix well together
                mix all together

Add:
    2 Cups Rolled oats (NOT instant)
    1 Pkg Choc. Chips.

    Bake @ 350F (177c) Approx 15 minutes
            Use Parchment Paper
                    Enjoy!

Mom's Biscochuelos

INGREDIENTS

Wet

½ cup margarine
2/3 vegetable shortening
1 egg

Dry

2 ½ cups flour (approx)
¼ cup corn meal
¼ tsp salt
¼ tsp baking powder
½ tsp cinnamon
1 tsp anise seed (or more)

DIRECTIONS

Cream margarine and shortening together. Add egg to mixture.
Add salt and spices, cornmeal and baking powder.
Gradually add flour and mix by hand until soft enough to roll.
Roll heaping teaspoon between hands and form into a ring.
Bake on a lightly greased cookie sheet for 10 min at 375 degrees.
Makes 5 dozen cookies.

NOTES

Baked cookies are best kept for a few days in a tightly covered container to develop the flavor.

Contributed by Cecilia Calderon

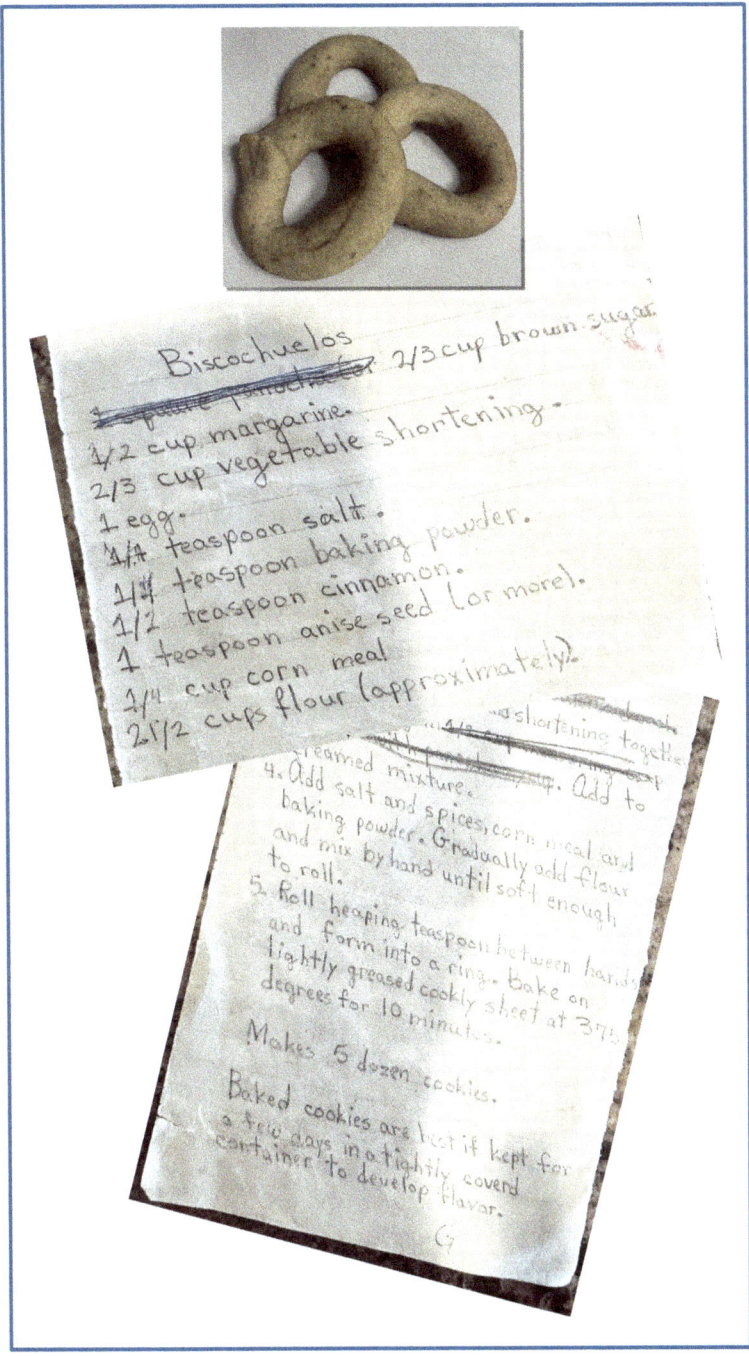

Biscochuelos

2/3 cup brown sugar

1/2 cup margarine.
2/3 cup vegetable shortening.
1 egg.
1/4 teaspoon salt.
1/4 teaspoon baking powder.
1/2 teaspoon cinnamon.
1 teaspoon anise seed (or more).
1/4 cup corn meal
2 1/2 cups flour (approximately).

shortening together
creamed mixture.
4. Add salt and spices, corn meal and
baking powder. Gradually add flour
and mix by hand until soft enough
to roll.
5. Roll heaping teaspoon between hands
and form into a ring. Bake on
tightly greased cookly sheet at 375
degrees for 10 minutes.

Makes 5 dozen cookies.

Baked cookies are best if kept for
a few days in a tightly coverd
container to develop flavor.

G

Bernies' Cherry Coconut Macaroon Cookies

INGREDIENTS

Wet

2/3 cup butter
¾ tsp vanilla
1 egg, beaten well

Dry

1 ¾ cups flour
1 tsp baking powder
½ tsp baking soda
½ cup chopped cherries
¾ cup sweetened coconut

DIRECTIONS

Cream well the butter, sugar, salt, vanilla.
Add beaten egg.
Combine dry ingredients. Add the combined wet ingredients.
Add the cherries and coconut.
Bake for 10-12 minutes at 370 degrees.

NOTES

Contributed by Monique Brockley Drinkman

Bernie's Cherry-Coconut Macaroon Cookies

370° 10-12 min.

Cream well —
2/3 c butter
3/4 C. sugar
1/2 tsp salt
3/4 tsp vanilla

add - beat well
1 egg   then add —
1 3/4 C flour
1 tsp baking powder
1/2 tsp soda.

add
1/2 c. chopped cherries
3/4 C. coconut

Orange Marmalade Cooky

INGREDIENTS

Wet

2 cups flour

1 tsp soda

1 tsp salt

Dry

1 cup marmalade

½ c shortening

1 egg beaten

DIRECTIONS

Mix all ingredients together and drop by tsp on baking sheet.
Bake for 10-12 minutes at 375 degrees.

NOTES

Contributed by Helene Robinson

Orange Marmalade Cooky

1 C. Orange Marmalade
1/2 C. Shortening
1 egg beaten
2 C. Flour   Drop by tsp.
1 tsp soda   Bake 10-12 mis @ 375°
1 tsp salt

Nannie's Hamentaschen

INGREDIENTS

Wet

1 cube butter
1 cup sour cream

Filling

1 can poppy seeds
½ cup dark chopped raisins
½ cup nuts

Dry

2 cups flour

Grated lemon rind

DIRECTIONS

Refrigerate mixture. Divide into quarters roll each quarter.
Flour rolling pin and top. Cut into circles. Fill with
heaping Tbsp filling. Place on greased cookie sheet and
bake for 10-15 minutes at 400 degrees, then lower to 350.
Makes 2 ½ - 3 dozen.

NOTES

My changes: make batter in food processor and use
margarine.
Use "Solo" brand fillings, available in kosher section at
store.
Do not overfill circles.
Bake for 25-30 minutes at 350 deg (instead of 400 then
lowering).
I use Pam spray on cookie sheet.

Contributed by Carla Winter, Photo by Judy Kaplan

Nannie's Hamentaschen

2 C flour
1 cake butter
1 cup sour cream
    Refrigerate mixture. Divide into quarters
and roll each quarter. Flour topas rolling
pin doc emp stick. Cut into circles. Fill
with heaping tbsp. filling, pinch.

Filling
    1 can poppy seeds
    1/2 C dark chopped raisins
    1/4 C nuts
    grated lemon rind

(over)

Place on greased cookie sheet In
400° oven for 10-15 min then lower
oven to 350°
    · 2 1/2 - 3 dozen
My changes: Make butter in food
            processor & use margarine
    · Use "Solo" filling available
        at store in kosher section
    · Do not overfill circles
    · Bake 350° 25-30 min
      (instead of 400° then cutting
        down)
    · I use "Pam" sprayed cookie
      sheet

Cocoa Kiss Cookies

INGREDIENTS

Wet

1 cup softened margarine
1 tsp vanilla extract

Dry

2/3 cup sugar
1 2/3 cup flour
¼ cup cocoa
1 cup finely chopped nuts
54 Hershey's Kisses - 9 oz
Confectioners sugar

DIRECTIONS

Mix and cream butter, sugar and vanilla until light and fluffy.
Combine flour and cocoa. Blend into creamed mixture.
Add nuts. Beat at low speed until blended.
Chill dough one hour until firm enough to handle.
Heat oven to 375 deg.
Mold scant Tbsp of dough around each Kiss, covering Kiss completely. Shape into balls.
Place on ungreased cookie sheet. Bake 10-12 minutes until almost set. Cool slightly; remove to wire rack. Cool completely, roll in powdered sugar. Makes 4 ½ dozen.

NOTES

Contributed by Tricia Clapp

Cocoa Kiss Cookies

1 cup margarine, softened	1 cup finely chopped nuts
²⁄₃ " sugar	54 Hershey Kisses - 9 oz.
1 Tsp. vanilla	Confectioners' sugar
1²⁄₃ cup flour	
¼ c. cocoa	

Mix + cream butter, sugar + vanilla until light and fluffy. Combine flour + cocoa blend into creamed mixture. Add nuts beat on low speed until blended.

Chill dough 1 hr. or until firm enough to handle. Heat oven to 375°. Mold about 1 Tblsp of dough around each Kiss, covering Kiss completely. Shape into balls; place on ungreased cookie sheet. Bake 10-12 min. or until almost set. Cool slightly; remove onto wire rack. Cool completely. Roll in powdered sugar. Makes 4½ dozen.

I didn't roll in powdered sugar -

Melamabarouna

INGREDIENTS

Wet

1 ¼ cup canola or other
neutral oil
1 cup orange juice
Grated rind of an orange
¼ cup whiskey or rum (or
agave if you prefer
vegetarian)

Dry

4 cups flour
1 tsp baking soda
1 tsp cinnamon
¼ tsp ground cloves
¾ cups chopped walnuts
(or omit if you are
allergic)

DIRECTIONS

Preheat oven to 375 degrees.

Whisk wet ingredients and sugar in a big bowl. Add dry
ingredients. Mix all together. Batter should be workable
but not too dry or too oily (add a little flour if it seems
too oily).

Form dough into round cakes about 1 ½ inches in
diameter and place on ungreased cookie sheet.

Bake for 15-25 minutes until toasty brown.

As they are finishing in the oven, bring 2-3 cups honey or
agave to a boil. As soon as the cookies come out of the
oven, give each a quick dip in the boiling honey/agave,
sprinkle with chopped walnuts if desired.

Cool on a wire rack.

Makes 32-33 cookies

Contributed by Nina Nelson

Melomakarouna

Recipe by: Nina Nelson
from her grandmother
Vasiliki Hianacopoulos

Makes 32-33 cookies

1¼ cups of oil (canola or another neutral oil)
½ cup sugar
1 cup orange juice
Grated rind of an orange
¼ cup whisky or rum
1 Tablespoon honey (or agave, if you want a vegan recipe)

Whisk wet ingredients in a big bowl. Or mix the dry ones first. It's a very forgiving recipe.

ADD:

4 cups flour
1 teaspoon baking soda
1 teaspoon cinnamon
¼ teaspoon ground cloves
¾ cups chopped walnuts (OPTIONAL — you can omit for people with nut allergies or just sprinkle them on top after dipping the cookies in hot honey or agave, or add them to the batter, as I do)

Preheat oven to 375°F. Mix all ingredients together. The consistency of the batter should be workable but not too dry or too oily — add a little flour if it seems too oily. Form dough into round cakes about 1½" in diameter and place on ungreased cookie sheet. Bake for 15-25 minutes until toasty brown.

As they are finishing in the oven, bring 2-3 cups of honey or agave to a boil. As soon as the cookies come out of the oven, give each one a quick dip in the boiling honey/agave, sprinkle with chopped walnuts, if desired, and let them cool on a wire rack.

Nina's Rum Balls

INGREDIENTS

1 cup semisweet chocolate chips
3 Tbsp light corn syrup
1 cup sugar (divided)
½ cup dark rum
¼ cup Kahlua
2 ½ cups finely chopped vanilla wafers (round 10 oz).
1 cup finely chopped walnuts

DIRECTIONS

Melt chocolate chips, either in the microwave or in the top of a double boiler over simmering water until smooth and completely melted. Whisk in ½ cup sugar, corn syrup, rum and Kahlua.

Mix vanilla wafers and walnuts in medium bowl, then add chocolate mixture and stir to blend well.

Put remaining ½ cup sugar in a shallow bowl. Roll one scant teaspoonful of the chocolate mixture into a 1" ball, then roll in sugar to coat evenly. Refrigerate at least overnight before serving.

They may be frozen–if they last that long!

NOTES

Ed. Note: having been the recipient of these amazing confections, I made a special request of Nina for the recipe. I've known her since she was a small child, so she didn't dare refuse. Besides, she's a kind and generous soul.

Contributed by Nina Nelson

Rum Balls

Recipe by: Nina Nelson
with a little help from
Epicurious.com

1 cup semisweet chocolate chips
1 cup sugar (divided use)
3 tablespoons light corn syrup
½ cup dark rum
¼ cup Kahlua
2½ cups finely chopped vanilla wafers (@ 10 oz., or a few cookies short of a box)
1 cup finely chopped walnuts

Melt chocolate chips, either in the microwave or in the top of a double boiler over simmering water, until smooth and completely melted. Whisk in ½ cup sugar, corn syrup, rum and Kahlua.

Mix vanilla wafers and walnuts in medium bowl, then add chocolate mixture and stir to blend well.

Remaining ½ cup of sugar will go in a shallow bowl. Roll one scant teaspoonful of the chocolate mixture into a 1" ball, then roll in sugar to coat evenly. Refrigerate at least overnight before serving. May also be frozen, if they last that long!

Peanut Butter Blossoms

INGREDIENTS

Wet

½ cup butter
1/3 cup peanut butter
1 unbeaten egg
1 tsp vanilla

Dry

1 ¾ cups flour
½ cup sugar
½ cup brown sugar
1 tsp soda
½ tsp salt

DIRECTIONS

(Ed. Note–as you can see, the directions are scant. My guess is, mix everything together and roll in sugar, bake for eight minutes at 375 deg., then put candy kisses on top and bake 2-5 minutes longer).

NOTES

This recipe is actually written on a cutting board.

Contributed by Ruth Holmes

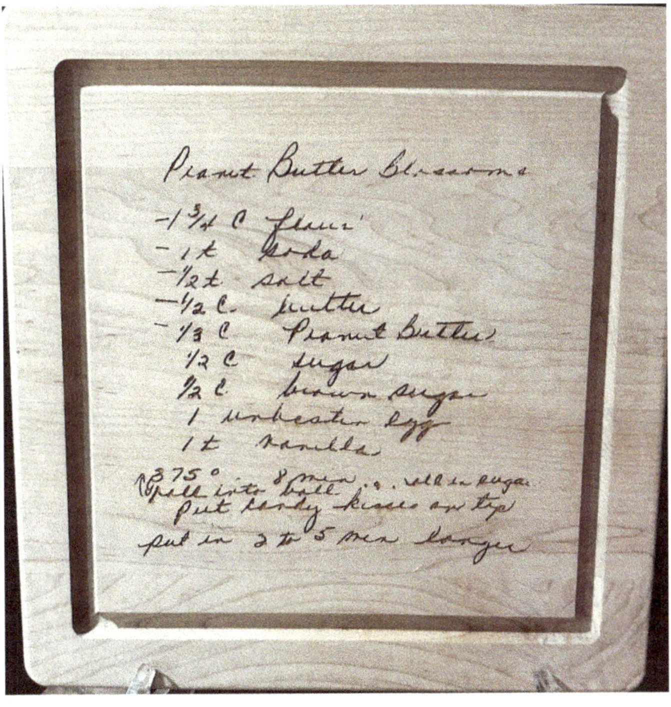

Peanut Butter Blossoms

- 1 ¾ C flour
- 1 t soda
- ½ t. salt
- ½ c. butter
- ⅓ C Peanut Butter
  ½ C sugar
  ½ C brown sugar
  1 unbeaten egg
  1 t vanilla

375°
Roll into ball . . . roll in sugar
put Hershy kisses on top
put in 2 to 5 min longer

Best Ever Spice Cookies

INGREDIENTS

Wet

¾ cup shortening
¼ cup molasses
1 unbeaten egg

Dry

2 cups flour
1 cup sugar
2 tsp soda
2 ½ tsp spice mixture
¼ tsp salt (optional)

DIRECTIONS

Mix wet ingredients together.
Sift together and stir in dry ingredients.
Mix all ingredients together. Shape into walnut-size balls.
Space two inches apart on a greased cookie sheet and
bake for 10-12 minutes at 375 degrees.

NOTES

Contributed by Ruth Holmes

Best Ever Spice Cookies

<u>Mix together</u>
3/4 cup shortening   1 unbeaten egg
1 cup Sugar   1/4 cup Molasses

<u>Sift together and stir in</u>
2 cups flour   2 t. soda
1/4 t. salt (optional)
2 1/2 t. spice mixture

Mix all ingredients together,
shape walnut-size balls.
Space two inches apart
on a greased cookie sheet
and bake at 375° for
10 to 12 minutes.

Teatime Tasties

INGREDIENTS

Wet

2 cream cheese (3 oz)
2 sticks oleo

Dry

2 cups flour

Filling

2 eggs, beaten
2 Tbsp melted butter
1 tsp vanilla
1 ¾ cup brown sugar
pinch of salt

DIRECTIONS

Cream together the cream cheese and oleo, then add the flour. Mix with hands and make into balls. Drop into small muffin tins and shape into crust with thumbs.

Filling
Mix filling ingredients together.
Place a few extra nuts in bottom of each tart and fill about ¾ full with filling.
Bake ½ hour at 350 degrees.

NOTES

(Ed. Note: there are no nuts listed in the ingredients, but are referred to in the directions. Use your judgment).

Contributed by Ruth Holmes

Makes 36 Teatime Tasties

2 3 oz Cr Cheese
2 Sticks Oleo
 Cream together and add : 3 c flr
Mix with hands and make into dough
drop into small muffin tins and shape
into crust with thumbs

Filling:
2 Eggs – beaten 1 3/4 c Br Sugar, well pa
1 t Vanilla   Pinch of salt
2 T Melted Butter
Pecans cut up

Place a few extra nuts in bottom of each tar
and fill about 3/4 full with filling.
Bake 1/2 hr 350°

Peg's Big Cookie

INGREDIENTS

Wet

3 Tbsp water
1 Tbsp peanut butter

Dry

1/3 cup dry milk
¾ oz dry cereal (oatmeal, rice crispies, fiber one)
2 Tbsp raisins
1 tsp cinnamon

DIRECTIONS

Mix ingredients together. Form one round cookie on greased baking sheet.
Bake 10-12 minutes at 350 degrees.

NOTES

Contributed by Peg Brantley; Photo by Judy Kaplan

Big Cookie _or 1 pckt_

⅓ c. dry milk Alba

3 T. water

1 T. peanut butter

2 T. raisins

1 t. cinnamon

¾ oz. dry cereal
(oatmeal, ricekrispies,
fiber one).

Mix together. Pam
cookie sheet. Make
one round cookie
on pan. Bake
350° 10 - 12 min.

1 cookie =
   1 milk
   1 bread
   1 fruit
   1 protein
   1 fat.

95

Mary's Pineapple Cookies

INGREDIENTS

Wet

1 cup shortening
1 egg
1 can (8 ¾ oz) crushed
pineapple with juice

Dry

3 ½ cup flour
1 cup sugar
1 tsp baking soda
½ tsp salt
¼ tsp nutmeg
½ cup nuts

DIRECTIONS

Cream shortening, sugar, and eggs. Add pineapple.
Blend dry ingredients and mix together.
Chill for 1 hour.
Ed note: some instructions may be missing. I think it
should say roll out and cut with cookie cutter.
Bake 8-10 minutes at 400 degrees.
Should make around 5 dozen.

NOTES

Mary was my mother's best friend and an amazing maker.
Of comfort food. They lived a few doors down from us,
and much of my misspent youth was as an unofficial part
of Mary's family, which included her parents, husband,
and daughter.

Contributed by Sheila Lowe

Pineapple Cookies

5 dz.

1 C shortening
1½ C sugar
1 egg
1 Can (8¾ 3) Pineapple crushed, juice
3½ C flour
1 t Soda   ¼ t nutmeg
½ t salt   ½ C nuts

cream short., & sugar & eggs. add pineapple
blend dry ingr. Chill 1 hour
Bake 8-10 min. @ 400°

Peanut Butter Balls

INGREDIENTS

Wet

1 stick margarine
2 cups peanut butter
3 cups Rice Krispies
1 bar (less than) paraffin

Dry

1 lbs (3 cups) powdered sugar
———-
1 large (8 oz) Hershey's milk chocolate bar
1 12 oz pkg chocolate chips

DIRECTIONS

Cream together the margarine, powdered sugar, peanut butter, Rice Krispies, (food processor works great) and form into balls.
Cream butter and peanut butter first, then add sugar and Krispies while forming into balls….
Melt in double boiler: chocolate bar, chips, paraffin. Using tongs, dip balls into chocolate. Place on waxed paper to cool.

NOTES

Contributed by Peg Brantley

Peanut Butter Balls

Cream & form
into balls:
- 1 cube margarine
- 1 lb (3 cups) powdered sugar
- 2 cups peanut butter
- 3 cups Rice Krispies

(Food Processor works great) — cream butter & P. Butter 1st then add sugar & Krispies

While forming into balls....
melt in double boiler)
- 1 lg. (8oz) Hershey's milk Chocolate bar
- 1 - 9oz pkg Chocolate chips
- 1 bar (less than) paraffin

Dip balls into Chocolate — using tongs.

Place on waxed paper to cool.

Serves: 150 balls

The Best of the Best Apple Pie

INGREDIENTS

Filling

2 Tbsp lemon juice
1 Tbsp apple cider vinegar
2/3 cup sugar
¼ cup unsalted butter
½ tsp ground cinnamon
½ tsp nutmeg
Pinch of salt

Crust

See next page

DIRECTIONS

Place oven rack on lower third of oven. Preheat to 325 deg. Prepare crust with top and bottom.

Peel and core apples, toss with apple cider and lemon. Melt butter over med-high heat. Add apples to skillet and cook, adding sugar and stir until dissolved. Lower heat to simmer 2 minutes. Cover and turn heat to med-low, cooking until apples soften and release most of juices (approximately 7 minutes).

Strain apples in colander over medium bowl, catch all juices. Return juices to skillet, simmer over medium heat thickened and lightly caramelized (approx. 10 minutes).

In a medium bowl, toss apples with reduced juices and spices. Set aside to cool. When completely cool, pour into prepared pastry crust. Drizzle with 2 Tbsp of whipping cream.

Put top crust on and brush with egg mixture–make 6 slits in top of crust. Refrigerate for 15 minutes. Bake on a baking sheet at 325 degrees until crust is golden brown (about 50 minutes) and cool.

Eat that thang!

Contributed by Linda Larson

The Best of The Best apple pie ... and
(it Really is!
[Follow the EXACT Instructions]

- Place oven Rack on lower third of The oven
- Preheat oven to 375° when ready to bake
- Prepare crust (both Top and bottom)

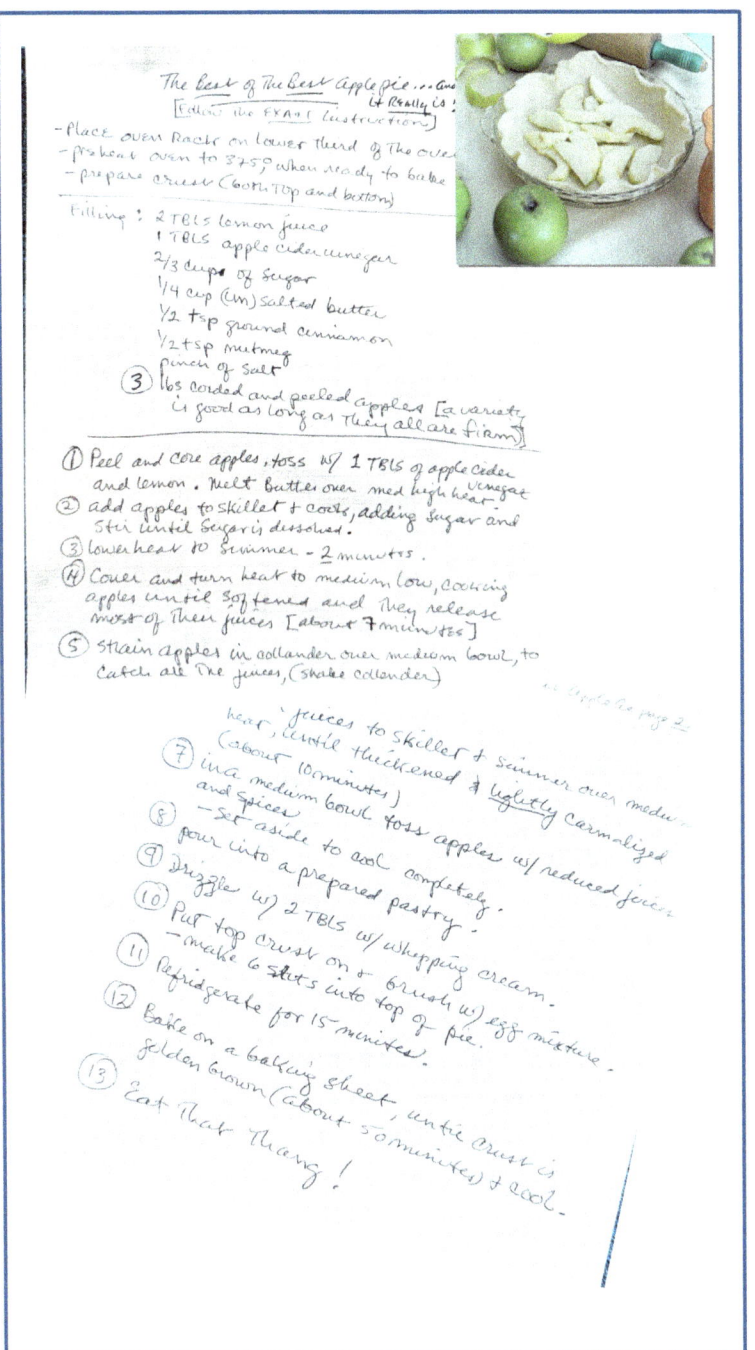

Filling:
- 2 TBLS lemon juice
- 1 TBLS apple cider vinegar
- 2/3 cups of sugar
- 1/4 cup (un)salted butter
- 1/2 tsp ground cinnamon
- 1/2 tsp nutmeg
- pinch of salt
- ③ lbs corded and peeled apples [a variety is good as long as They all are firm]

① Peel and core apples, toss w/ 1 TBLS of apple cider and lemon. Melt butter over med high heat. vinegar
② add apples to skillet + cook, adding sugar and stir until sugar is dissolved.
③ lower heat to simmer - 2 minutes.
④ Cover and turn heat to medium low, cooking apples until softened and They release most of Their juices [about 7 minutes]
⑤ Strain apples in collander over medium bowl, to catch all The juices, (shake colender)

on Apple pie page 2

⑥ heat' juices to skillet + simmer over medium, until thickened + lightly carmalized (about 10 minutes)
⑦ in a medium bowl toss apples w/ reduced juices and spices
⑧ - set aside to cool completely.
⑨ pour into a prepared pastry.
⑩ Drizzle w/ 2 TBLS w/ whipping cream.
⑪ Put top crust on + brush w/ egg mixture.
- make 6 sluts into top of pie.
⑫ Refridgerate for 15 minutes.
⑬ Bake on a baking sheet, until crust is golden brown (about 50 minutes) + cool.
Eat That Thang!

Pie Crust that Works!

INGREDIENTS

Wet

1 cup lard (Crisco has a
better flavor)
6-8 Tbsp cold water

Dry

3 cups all-purpose flour
¼ tsp salt

This recipe makes a
two-crust pie

DIRECTIONS

Mix flour and salt, cut in lard until crumbly.
Shape into a disk, wrap and refrigerate 1one hour to
overnight.
On a lightly floured surfaced, roll into two 1/8" thick
circles. Transfer to pie plate. Fill crust, place second circle
on top and crimp the edges to seal. Use a fork or knife to
poke holes in the top crust to allow steam to escape while
baking.

NOTES

Forever, I had not been able to make a pie crust that I
would end up piecing the crust together with my thumb,
which always looked terrible but tasted okay. So this
recipe is the first that allowed me to make a classic pie. I
was thrilled!

Contributed by Linda Larson

A PIE CRUST THAT WORKS!

Forever, I had not been able to make a pie crust that. I would end up piecing the crust together w/my thumb always looked terrible, but tasted OK. So this recipe is the first that allowed me to make a classic pie cr I was thrilled!

Lard Pie Crust

3 cups all purpose flower
1/4 teaspoon of salt
1 cup of LARD (CRISCO has a nice Butter flavor)
6-8 TABLESPOON Cold Water

- Mix flour & salt, cut in lard, until crumbley
- shape into a disk, wrap & Refrigerate 1 hour over night.
- On a lightly floured surfaced surface.
- Roll into 1/8" Thick circle.
- Transfer to pie plate.

Mother's Never Fail Pie Crust

INGREDIENTS

Wet

1 ½ cups shortening
3 ½ Tbsp cold water
1 egg, beaten
1 T vinegar

Dry

3 cups flour
1 tsp salt

DIRECTIONS

Mix flour, salt, shortening with pastry blender.
Beat the egg and add vinegar and water. Combine with flour and shortening mix.
Roll out and place in pie tin. Bake for 12-14 minutes at 450 degrees.

NOTES

(Ed. Note: this is a double crust recipe)

Contributed by Jane O'Brien

Never Fail - Pie Crust.   450°
                          12 - 14 min.
3 cups flour.
1 tsp salt
1½ c. shortening
Mix ē pastry blender—
{ Beat 1 egg → add
{ 1 T. vinegar
{ 3½ T. cold H_2O
  Add to flour + shortening mixt

107

Honey Pumpkin Pie

INGREDIENTS

Wet

1 ½ cups cooked pumpkin
2/3 cup honey
1 cup evaporated milk

Dry

½ tsp salt
½ tsp cinnamon, ginger
¾ tsp vanilla extract

DIRECTIONS

Combine pumpkin, honey, cinnamon, vanilla, salt. Add eggs and evaporated milk.

Pour into unbaked pie shell.
(Ed. Note: no time or temperature given. Suggested by Google: Bake a honey pumpkin pie by first preheating the oven to 425°F for 15 minutes, then lowering the temperature to 350°F and baking for another 40-60 minutes, or until the center is set. A knife inserted near the center should come out clean.

NOTES

Contributed by Carla Winter

Honey Pumpkin Pie
1 1/3 cups Cooked Pumpkin
2/3 cup honey
2 eggs
1 cup Evaporated milk
1/2 tsp salt
1/2 tsp Cinnamon - Ginger
1/4 tsp vanilla
        Unbaked pie shell
   Combine pumpkin, honey, cinnamon,
vanilla, + salt. add eggs + milk.

Jackie Olden's Carrot Pie

INGREDIENTS

Wet

2 cups cooked, pureed
carrots
¾ cup evaporated milk
3 eggs, beaten

Dry

1 cup brown sugar or honey
½ tsp salt
1 tsp cinnamon
½ tsp nutmeg
½ tsp ginger
1/8 tsp cloves

DIRECTIONS

Combine all ingredients except the eggs. Then add them.
Pour into an unbaked pie shell and bake for 40-45
minutes at 400 deg.

NOTES

Eons ago, when I was first married (20 years old), I
listened to cooking shows on the radio. Jackie Olden, who
was the author of numerous cookbooks, was one of my
favorites. This is her recipe for carrot pie. It's a lot like
pumpkin pie.

(don't judge my immature handwriting!)

Contributed by Sheila Lowe

Carrot Pie   Jackie
                                     Olde
2 C pureed cooked Carrots
1 C brn Sug. or honey   )
3/4 C evap. milk
                                } Combine
1/2 t. Salt
1 t. Cinnamon
1/2 t. nutmeg.
1/2 t. ginger
1/8 t cloves
add 3 eggs, beaten.   400°
              unbaked pie shell Bake 40-45m

Lemon Pie

INGREDIENTS

Wet

1 cup milk
3 egg yolks
Juice and rind of one lemon

Dry

1 cup sugar
3 Tbsp flour
¼ tsp salt

DIRECTIONS

Mix sugar, flour, salt. Beat egg yolks well and add milk.
Add dry ingredients.
Cook in double boiler until thick, stirring well. Add
lemon and rind after removing from heat.
Pour into baked pie shell.
Meringue: Beat egg whites until stiff and add 3 Tbsp
sugar.
Cover pie with meringue.
Bake in oven until meringue is light brown.
This can be used with chocolate or banana filling. Add
vanilla instead of lemon.

NOTES

Ed note: No temperature or time given. Google says bake
for 20-25 minutes at 325 degrees. If you are adding a
meringue topping, add meringue and bake for another 15
minutes at 350 degrees until the meringue is golden
brown.

Contributed by Ruth Holmes

Lemon Pie

1 C sugar
1 C milk
3 egg yolks
3 T flour
1/4 tsp salt
juice & rind one lemon

Mix sugar & flour & salt. Beat egg yolks
well & add milk. Add dry ingredients.

Cook in double boiler til thick, stirring
well. Add lemon & rind after removing from heat. Pour in cooked baked
pie shell. Beat egg whites til stiff
& add 3 T sugar. Bake in oven til
meringue is light brown.
This filling can be used as chocolate
filling or banana. Add vanilla instead of lemon.

The Best Avocado Pie

INGREDIENTS

Crust

5 Tbsp unsalted butter, melted
1 ½ cups graham cracker crumbs
1 Tbsp granulated sugar
Pinch of salt

Filling

2 medium ripe avocados, peeled, seeded, mashed
1 10 oz can sweetened condensed milk
1 8 oz pkg cream cheese, room temperature
2 Tbsp fresh lime juice
Pinch of salt

DIRECTIONS

Crust: brush 9" spring form pan w/spray or melted butter. Press mix into bottom and up sides of pan. Bake 15 minutes at 350 deg.
Filling: blend avocado, condensed milk, cream cheese, lime juice, lemon juice in a blender until smooth.
Pour into prepared pie crust. Refrigerate at least 30 minutes.
Top with whipped cream.

NOTES

Weird, but wonderful!

Contributed by Linda Larson

Submitted by
Linda Larson

The Best Avacado Pie – weird, but wonderful!

Crust: Oven 350°

5 TBLS unsalted butter melted

1½ cup graham cracker crumbs

1 TBLS granulated sugar

Punch of Salt

Brush 9" Spring pan w/ Pam Spray or melted butter.
Press mix into bottom & up the sides.
Bake 15 minutes

Filling: 2 medium ripe avacados, peeled, seeded & mashed

1 (10oz) can sweetended condensed milk

1 (8oz) pkg cream cheese, at room temp

2 TBLS lime juice (Fresh)

1½ TBLS lemon juice (Fresh)

punch salt

- Blend Avacado, Sweetened condensed milk, cream cheese, lime juice & lemon juice in a blender until smooth.

- pour into prepared pie crust

- Refrigerate for at least 30 minutes

- Top w/ whipped cream

115

Melktert (Milk Tart)

DIRECTIONS

Sweet pastry

Cream together 2 oz butter and 2 ½ tsp granulated sugar
2 ½ tsp oil. Add the following:

1 cup flour

1 tsp baking powder

½ egg

Press into greased pie dish. Bake for 15 minutes at 350
degrees.

Filling

Boil together:

2 cups milk

¼ cup butter

1 cinnamon stick

Mix together:

2 eggs

½ cup sugar

vanilla

5 tsp

3 tsp maizena (cornstarch)

salt

Add to boiling mixture. Return to stove, stirring all the
time until thick. Pour into cooked crust and sprinkle with
cinnamon.

NOTES

Contributed by Terry Elmaleh (South Africa)

MELKTERT

Sweet Pastry.

2 oz butter
12,5 ml castor sugar } cream
2,5 oil
250 ml flour
5 ml baking powder
½ egg

Press into greased piedish. Bake 350° (180°) for 15 minutes

Filling
500 ml milk
60 ml butter } boil together
1 cinnamon stick

Mix together:
2 eggs
25 ml sugar
vanilla

25 ml flour
12,5 ml maizena
salt

Then add to boiling mixture. Put back on stove stirring all the time until thick. Pour into dish. Sprinkle with cinnamon.

Chess Pie

INGREDIENTS

Wet

4 eggs
¼ cup melted butter
¼ cups sweet milk
¼ cup lemon juice
Grated rind of 2 lemons

Dry

2 cups sugar
2 Tbsp cornmeal
1 Tbsp flour

DIRECTIONS

Mix first sugar and cornmeal, add eggs one at a time. Stir in butter, milk, lemon juice and rind.
Pour into unbaked pie shell and bake for about 45 minutes at 350 degrees.
Cool before cutting.

NOTES

Contributed by Lib Porter via Helene Robinson

HERE'S WHAT'S COOKING: Chess Pie

FROM THE KITCHEN OF: LIB PORTER PICKENS, SC

2 C. sugar	½ C. melted butter
2 T. cornmeal	½ C. sweet milk
1 T. flour	¼ C. lemon juice
4 Eggs	grated rind of 2 lemons

Mix first 3 ingredients, add eggs one at a time, stir in butter, milk, lemon juice & rind. Pour into unbaked pie shell and bake at 350° for about 45 minutes. Cool before cutting.

Chuck's Famous Fudge

INGREDIENTS

Wet

15 oz can evaporated milk
2 capfuls real vanilla or
chocolate essence

* Start with a glass of
Bailey's or Kahlua for the
chef (optional!)

Dry

8 oz. Semisweet
morsels
8 oz Trader Joe's
chocolate covered
espresso beans (adjust
to taste)
Pinch of sea salt

DIRECTIONS

Place morsels and beans in a large nonstick pan. Add salt,
milk. Melt over low heat, stirring occasionally. Add
vanilla. Optional: ½ - ¾ chopped nuts. Mix well.
Line a baking sheet with parchment paper. Pour fudge
onto the paper, cover with a second sheet of parchment.
Roll enough to make it ½ - ¾" thick. Cool in fridge or
freezer. When solid, cut into squares.
Pastosity in culinary form!

NOTES

Kahlil Gibran wrote that a marriage begins with a *glance*
and ends in eternity, (optimistically). My fudge recipe
comes from the back of a cocoa package, also *glanced* at.
"Fool-proof" was a big attraction. It has evolved each
year in trying various additions, including Trader Joe's
chocolate-covered espresso beans. My late brother, Jim,
liked to say that 'there is no X in espresso." *Enjoy!*

Contributed by Charles Talmadge

Chuck's Famous Fudge

"Ruining appetites since 1982"

Start with a glass of Bailey's or Kahlua.

— optional —

for the chef.

Add the following in a non-stick lg pan:

{ 8 oz. Semisweet morsels —

{ 8 oz. Trader Joe's Chocolate Covered
espresso beans®. Adjusted to taste.

Pinch of sea salt

14 oz. can sweetened condensed milk.

Melt over low heat — stirring occas.

Add 2 capfuls of real vanilla or choc.

essence.

Optional — 1/2 - 3/4 c walnuts (or pecans)

Mix well —

Line a baking sheet with parchment paper
to cover. Pour fudge on to the paper,
cover it with a second sheet parchment.
Roll enough to make it 1/2" - 3/4" thick —
Cool in fridge or freezer.

when solid, cut into lines, then squares

Pastosity in Culinary form.

Ribbon Mold

INGREDIENTS

Wet

1 cup pineapple juice
1 cup crushed pineapple
1 cup hot water
1 cup mayonnaise
1 packet Dream Whip

Dry

1 cup marshmallows
1 8 oz pkg cream cheese

Separately prepare a box of cherry jello and lemon jello in molds. When set, place one on top of the other.

DIRECTIONS

Bottom layer: make cherry jello according to pkg. Set.
Middle layer: lemon jello according to pkg. Set.
Top layer: Blend hot water and marshmallows.
Whip pineapple juice and cream cheese and add to mixture.
Fold in mayonnaise and Dream Whip.
Refrigerate and set in mold. Place on top of the other two.

NOTES

Contributed by Tamara Tazzia

Ribbon Mold

Bottom   cherry
Middle   lemon jello

blend { 1 c. hot water
{ 1 c. marshmallows

add { 1 c. pineapple jucy
whip { 1 pack. 8 oz cream cheese

stir in   1 c. crushed pineapple

fold in   1 c. salad dressing.
      1 pack. dream whip

Lemon Sponge Custard

INGREDIENTS

Wet

1 ½ cups milk
4 Tbsp lemon juice
3 eggs, separated
2 Tbsp butter
1 Tbsp lemon rind

Dry

1 cup sugar
4 Tbsp flour
Dash salt

DIRECTIONS

Cream sugar and butter, add dry ingredients. Stir in beaten egg yolk with milk and lemon juice.
Beat eggs whites until stiff. Fold into the rest.
Fill lightly greased custard cups 2/3 full with mixture.
Set in pan, fill pan with hot water to 1 inch.
Bake for 45 minutes at 325 degrees.

NOTES

Important: After beating the egg yolks, be sure to use a clean, dry beater for the egg whites.

Contributed

Lemon Sponge Custard
Grandma Clark, Stetson, ME

1 C Sugar	3 eggs, separated
5 T Lemon Juice	2 T butter
4 T Flour	1 T lemon rind
Dash Salt	1½ C Milk

Cream sugar + butter. Add rest of dry ingredients. Stir in beaten egg yolk, with milk + lemon juice.

Beat egg whites till stif. Fold into rest.
 Fill lightly greased custard cups ⅔ full with mixture. Set in 9x13 Pan. Fill Pan with hot water to 1"
Bake at 325° for 45 min.

Mississippi Mud

INGREDIENTS

Wet

¾ cup margarine
3 cups milk
8 oz cream cheese
1 cup Cool Whip

Dry

1 ½ cup flour
1/3 cup nuts
2 pkg instant chocolate pudding.
¾ cup powdered sugar

DIRECTIONS

Mix the margarine, flour and nuts. Spread in 9 x 13 pan. Bake ten minutes at 350 deg. Let cool.

Cream cheese layer: mix Cool Whip, powdered sugar, and cream cheese and spread on 1st layer. Sprinkle with nuts.

Prepare the instant pudding with the milk, beat until smooth. Spread over cream cheese layer. Cover pudding layer with 9 oz of Cool Whip. Sprinkle with nuts.

NOTES

Contributed by Jane O'Brien

Mississippi Mud

3/4 c marg
1 1/2 c flour
1/3 c. nuts
Mix & put in 9x13 - Bake 350°
  10 min - Cool
Next take, 1 c Cool Whip, 3/4 c powd.
sugar & 8 oz cm. cheese. Mix &
put on 1st layer. Sprinkle w
  nuts.

2 pkgs choc. inst. pudding, add
3 c milk, beat 'til smooth.
Spread over cream cheese layer.
Cover pudding layer w 9 oz
Cool Whip. Sprinkle w nuts.

 Dirt Dessert

INGREDIENTS

Wet

1 pkg cream cheese (8 oz)
3 ½ cups milk
1 carton Cool Whip
¼ stick oleo or butter

Dry

1 pkg Oreo cookies
(crushed)
¼ cup powdered sugar
2 pkg instant French
vanilla pudding

DIRECTIONS

Cream oleo, cream cheese, powdered sugar.
Prepare pudding with milk as directed on package.
Combine with above.
Place half of crushed cookies in bottom of pot and rest
on top. Add a flower (I wrapped stems in foil or saran
wrap).

NOTES

Contributed by Tamara Tazzia - Kay Van Wormer, her mom

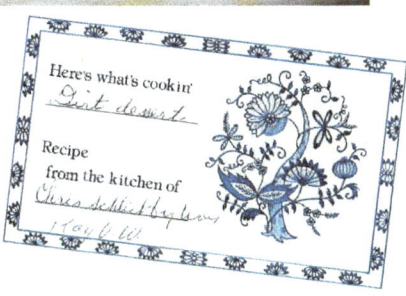

Here's what's cookin'
Dirt dessert

Recipe
from the kitchen of
Chris Schlichtig (my
Kay) 6/10

1 pkg. Oreo cookies (crushed)
1/4c. stick oleo or butter
1 pkg. 8oz cream cheese
1/4 c. powdered sugar
3 1/2 c milk
2 pkgs (instant) French Vanilla Pudding
1 carton (12oz) cool whip

cream oleo, cream cheese, & powdered sugar
together, combine (Pudding & milk)
as on direction's. combine with
above)
Place half of crushed cookies in
bottom of pot & rest on top - add
flowers -
(I wrapped stems in foil
or saran wrap.

Yugoslavian Gansa

INGREDIENTS

Wet

1-2 eggs

Milk to make a thick batter

Frying oil

Dry

2 cups flour

1 tsp salt

½ tsp baking powder

DIRECTIONS

Combine all ingredients to a thick, pancake-like batter.
Fry in oil, stirring constantly with knives until chunky and lightly browned.
Serve in a bowl. Pour coffee over it if you wish, and add sugar and/or cream.

NOTES

This Gansa recipe came from my great-grandma, who came to the US from Italy for an arranged marriage. Her two brothers living in the US were reputed to be associated with the dictator, Tito. Besides cooking, g-grandma also taught me some Yugoslavian curse words. She was one of the first women I'd ever seen wearing pants, and who made homemade wine and beer to trade for whatever.

Contributed by Peg Brantley

Gansa
2 c flour
1-2 eggs
1 t. salt
1/2 t. baking powder
milk to make thick batter
fry in oil with knives constantly
stirring

Nutella Crepe

INGREDIENTS

Wet

2 eggs
3 Tbsp butter
1 ½ cups milk
Nutella
Bananas

Dry

1 ¼ - 1 ½ cups sifted
flour
2 Tbsp
Pinch of salt

DIRECTIONS

Beat flour, eggs, butter and milk into a batter. Add salt
and sugar.
Pour mixture in heated crepe pan to cover.
Spread Nutella on top (optional)
Add sliced bananas (optional)
That's it!

NOTES

This delightful recipe came from a student of Maria Lam.

Contributed by Berenice Ng (Hong Kong)

NUTELLA
CREPE

(.50g)

FLOUR

SIFT THE
FLOUR

(2 eggs)
EGG

40g /
(3 Tbsp)

PINCH of SALT
&
SUGAR
(2 tbsp)

(375ml)

MILK

PLACE THE
PAN
ON THE HEAT

DONE

NUTELLA

SPREAD
NUTELLA
(optional)

(optional)
PLACE
SLICED
BANANA

1. beat the flour, eggs butter and milk into a batter.
2. remember to add sugar and salt
3. after mixing
4. heat the batter in a frying pan
5. spread the nutella on top
6. add sliced bananas

That's it!

Chocolate Bar

INGREDIENTS

Wet

¼ lb butter
1 egg yolk
1 tsp vanilla extract

Dry

1 ¼ cup flour
1 tsp baking powder
½ cup sugar
1 Tbsp cocoa
Dash of salt

DIRECTIONS

Mix all ingredients together and fill two loaf pans. Press down to ¼".
Brush with beaten egg white and sprinkle with sugar and/or almonds.
Bake for about 15 minutes at 350 degrees.
Cool before cutting into bars.

NOTES

Ed note: the recipe doesn't call for frosting, but there's no reason not to use it if you want to.

Contributed by Ruth Holmes

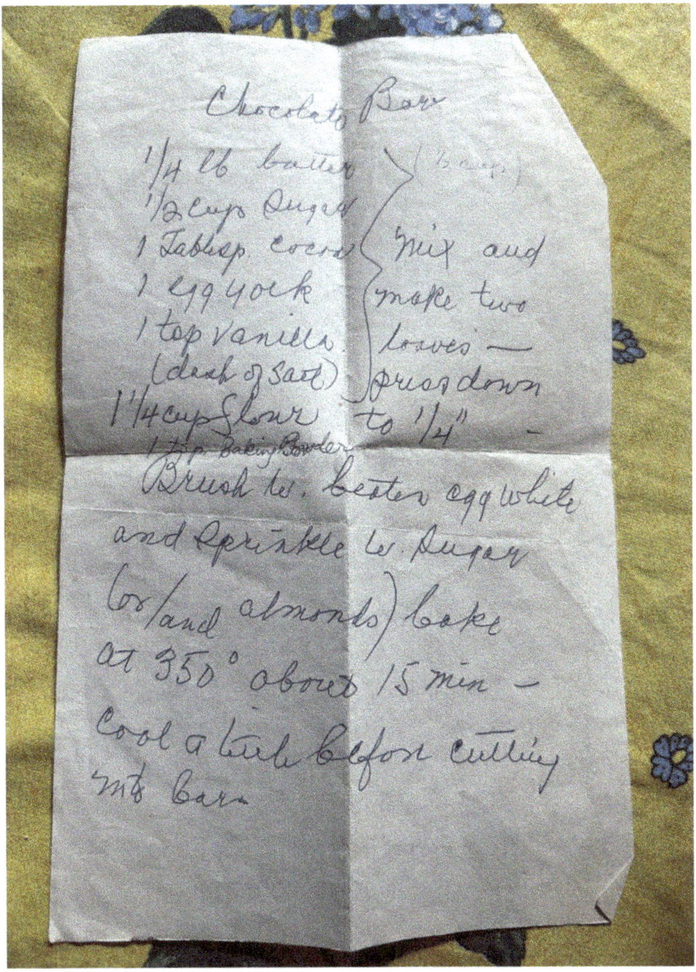

Chocolate Bars

1/4 lb butter ⎫ (1 cup)
1/2 cup sugar ⎪
1 Tablsp cocoa ⎬ mix and
1 egg yolk ⎪ make two
1 tsp vanilla ⎪ loaves —
(dash of salt) ⎭ press down
1 1/4 cup flour to 1/4" —
1 tsp Baking Powder

Brush w. beaten egg white
and sprinkle w. sugar
(or/and almonds) bake
at 350° about 15 min —
Cool a little before cutting
into bars

Chocolate Cottage Pudding
& Foamy Sauce

INGREDIENTS

Wet

2 Tbsp butter
½ tsp vanilla extract
1/8 tsp salt
1 egg
6 Tbsp milk

Dry

½ cup sugar
¾ cup bread flour (sift
before measuring)
Re-sift with 2 Tbsp
cocoa
¼ tsp salt
1 tsp baking powder

DIRECTIONS

Mix together wet ingredients. Add sifted ingredients with
milk. Pour into greased muffin cups. Bake 20 min. at 350
deg. Serve with Foamy Sauce

Foamy Sauce
Sift 1 cup powdered sugar.
Beat until soft: 5 Tbsp to ½ cup butter. Add sugar slowly.
Beat until well blended. Beat in egg yolk and vanilla. Place
sauce over hot beater, beat and cook until yolk has
thickened slightly.
Whip until stiff: egg white and salt. Fold lightly into sauce.
Serve hot or cold.

Contributed by Ruth Holmes

Chocolate Cottage Pudding

½ c. sugar
2 tbs. butter
½ tsp. vanilla
1 egg

Sift before measuring
3/4 c. bread flour
Resift with
2 tbsp. cocoa
¼ tsp. salt
1 tsp. baking powder

Add sifted ingredients to sugar mixture w/
6 tbsp. milk. → In greased muffin cups
Bake 20 min. @ 350°. Serve w/ foamy sauce.

Foamy Sauce (about 2 cupfulls)

Sift 1 c powdered sugar
Beat until soft: 5 tbsp to ½ c butter
Add sugar slowly. Beat these ingredients
until they are well-blended.
Beat in: 1 egg yolk
1 teaspoon vanilla

Place sauce over hot water. Beat + cook it
until the yolk has thickened slightly. Whip until
stiff: 1 egg white ⅛ tsp. salt
Fold it lightly into sauce. Serve hot or cold.

Fabulous Fudge Sauce

INGREDIENTS

Wet

1 cup evaporated milk
1 Tbsp butter
1 tsp vanilla extract

Dry

4 oz unsweetened chocolate
1 ½ cups sugar
Pinch of cream of tartar
Pinch of salt

DIRECTIONS

In double boiler melt chocolate, add sugar, cream of tartar, and salt. Gradually stir in milk. Cook until thick, about ten minutes. Cool slightly, then stir in vanilla and butter.

NOTES

Contributed by Ruth Holmes

Fabulous Fudge Sauce
4 oz. unsweetened chocolate
1½ C granulated sugar
pinch cream of tartar
pinch of salt
1 C+ evaporated milk
1 T butter
1 t vanilla-

In double boiler melt chocolate, add sugar, cream of tartar & salt - Gradually stir in milk- Cook until thick about 10 minutes. Cook slightly stir vanilla & butter.

Bananas Hawaiian

INGREDIENTS

Wet

3 Tbsp butter
1 cup dark rum
6 bananas, sliced

2 quarts vanilla ice cream

Dry

¾ cup coconut
½ cup packed brown sugar
¼ tsp cinnamon

DIRECTIONS

Heat coconut in skillet until toasted. Brown evenly and cool on foil.

Add butter, sugar, rum, cinnamon to skillet. Heat to bubbly. Add bananas, heat through.

Spoon bananas and juice over ice cream, sprinkle with coconut. Serve immediately

NOTES

Contributed by Sheila Lowe

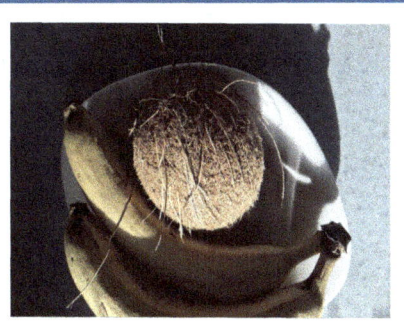

Bananas Hawaiian
Serves 8

3/4 C. Coconut
3 T butter
1/2 C. packed br. sugar
1 C dark rum
1/4 t. gr. Cinnamon
6 Bananas, sliced
2 Qts Vanilla ice cream

Heat coconut till toasted. Brown evenly
Cool on foil.
Add butter, sugar, rum, cinnamon
to skillet. Heat til bubbly. Add bananas
Heat through.
Spoon bananas & juice over ice cream
Sprinkle w/ coconut. Serve immediately

143

Harvey Wallbanger Sherbet

INGREDIENTS

Wet

2 cups milk
1 cup cream
1 cup fresh orange juice
3 Tbsp vodka
3 Tbsp Galliano
2 Tbsp lemon juice
Pinch of salt

Dry

1 cup sugar

DIRECTIONS

Heat the milk with the sugar until the sugar dissolves.
Add the remaining ingredients and blend thoroughly.
Pour into a tray and freeze. Stir when crystals form, then
freeze again.

NOTES

The perfect go-with for that Harvey Wallbanger cake,
found elsewhere in this book.

Contributed by Sheila Lowe

mitu Roy   Wallbanger Sherbet

2 C milk   } heat til sug. dissolves
1 C sugar. }

add 1 C cream
     1 C fresh O.J.
     3 T vodka
     3 T Galliano
     2 T lem Jc
     Pinch Salt.

Blend. pour into tray. Freeze - stir when
crystals form. Freeze again.

145

Pollo alla Parmigiana

INGREDIENTS

Chicken Parmesan cutlets

2 chicken breasts each cut into half sized portions (all fat and or tendon removed), each sliced in half-sized portions, resulting in 4 cutlets
2 eggs
1 cup of Italian Seasoned Breadcrumbs
Extra light olive oil for frying
3 slices of thinly sliced fresh mozzarella
1 teaspoon of Parmigiano Reggiano
1 teaspoon of Pecorino Romano

Marinara Sauce

1 can of San Marzano tomatoes (28 oz)
3 cloves of finely minced garlic
¼ tsp of dried oregano
Handful of fresh basil leaves
Good quality Olive Oil (enough to coat bottom of pan)
Italian Sea Salt and Red Pepper Flakes to Taste

INSTRUCTIONS

1) Trim cutlets of all fat, tendon or bloody bits. You can pound them thinner under a mallet to achieve a thinner and more uniform thickness.
2) Crack two eggs and beat in a bowl
3) Submerge cutlets first in egg wash, suspend them until excess egg wash drips off into bowl, and dredge in a shallow dish with evenly dispersed Italian bread crumbs.

Contributed by Anthony Brochetelli

Make sure to cover all sides of the cutlet so there are no empty patches.

4) Pour enough extra light olive oil into shallow pan just enough to coat the bottom of a pan. You can place all breaded cutlets in the pan even before any of it gets heated.

5) After all cutlets are

in pan gradually start to heat everything on a medium flame.

6) Fry each cutlet at least five minutes per side until cooked through. Center should not be gray but must be white.

7) Place cooked cutlets on steel tray. Ladle a few tablespoons of marinara sauce on top of each cutlet. Grate a little Parmesan and Pecorino cheese on top. Place a thin slice of fresh mozzarella on top of each. Then ladle a few more tablespoons of sauce thinly on top over the mozzarella. Place under the broiler for about 10 minutes. Remove promptly and serve when at ideal temperature.

8) Garnish with fresh washed basil leaves to beautify presentation if using basil (or fresh chopped parsley).

Handwritten recipe appears on the next page

Pollo alla Parmigiana

Pollo alla Parmigiana

Ingredients
For Chicken Cutlets
- 2 chicken breasts each cut in half
- ½ cup flour
- 2 eggs
- 1 cup of Italian Seasoned Bread Crumbs
- Extra Light Olive oil for frying
- 3 slices of thinly sliced fresh mozzarella
- 1 tsp of Parmigiano Reggiano e
  1 tsp of Pecorino Romano

For Marinara Sauce
- 1 28 oz can of San Marzano Tomatoes
- 3 cloves of finely minced garlic
- ¼ tsp of dried oregano
- Handful of fresh Basil leaves
- Good quality Olive Oil
- Italian Sea Salt and Red Pepper
- Flakes to taste!

151

Chicken Tetrazzini

Ingredients

4 cups rice
1 can cream of celery soup
3 little pkg chopped chives
Mushrooms (lots)
Chicken broth
Cheddar or Romano cheese (whole 8 oz pkg)
Chicken - cut up fryer, de-boned in large pieces
Far(?) chopped pimiento

Directions

Combine soup and broth, mix well. Heat to boiling.
Remove from heat, add chives, mushrooms, stir well.
Put in casserole or any buttered baking dish.
Sprinkle pimiento on top. Bake for 30 minutes at 350
degrees.
Serves 4-6

NOTES

When I first migrated to the Bay Area from LA back in
'75, I lived in a cooperative house in Piedmont with 3-5
residents, which changed from time to time. Ed Hall was
in his late twenties, a thin, dark stringy hair and was
working on his PhD in sex. He loved to cook and this is a
recipe sent from a friend of his.

Contributed by Carla Winter

Ed, Here is the Chicken tetrazzini recipe
Ingredients
4 cups rice
1 can cream of celery soup
1 can cream mushroom soup
3 little pkgs chopped chives
mushrooms (lots
chicken broth

cheddar or romano cheese
(whole pkg) 8 oz
Chicken (cut-up fryer or
leave in large pcs.
but debone.
jar chopped pimento

Combine soup + broth, mix well. Heat to boiling
Remove from heat. add chives, mushrooms + cheese
stir til cheese has melted mix in chicken + stir up
Put in casserole or any baking dish (butter the
baking dish). Sprinkle pimento on top. Bake at
350° for 30 minutes. The recipe book says
serves 8 but it doesn't (more like 4-6). Love
Kan

Karen Goldberger
c/o Crestview Dr
Richardson, ???

IN BOUND
OCT 18
PM
1974
5290

Samuel Adams Patriot
U.S. Postage 8¢

Ed Hill
416 Pala
Redmont, Calif
94611

153

Penne ala Vodka

INGREDIENTS

1 28 oz can of San Marzano tomatoes (crush them by hand in a bowl afterwards)

1 cup of heavy cream (organic is the best)

½ cup of Pecorino Romano Cheese

½ cup of Parmigiano Reggiano Cheese

½ of one Vidalia Onion finely chopped

3 cloves of finely chopped garlic

½ teaspoon of crushed red pepper flakes (optional)

Handful of fresh basil leaves

½ cup of vodka (optional)

½ can of tomato paste

Penne pasta, preferable from Gragnano

1 Tbsp of Calabrian Chili Paste (if you like it hot and spicy)

INSTRUCTIONS

Put enough olive oil into saucepan enough to evenly coat bottom.

Add in 1 very finely chopped Vidalia onion.

When onion starts to turn a golden brown color but is not burnt, add finely chopped garlic before onion is completely cooked through, as well as ½ can of tomato paste and pinch of hot pepper flakes, breaking up the tomato paste into the mixture.

Contributed by Anthony Brochetelli

When onion and garlic are completely caramelized in pan, remove the pan from the flame and safely add cup of vodka when completely away from flame. Let vodka reduce in pan over low heat for a few minutes and then add in the hand-crushed San Marzano tomatoes.

Let tomato sauce simmer down for about 15 minutes. After 15 minutes, add in heavy cream and cup of grated cheese blend. Let cook for an additional 10 minutes or so.

When Penne pasta is 95 % cooked, remove from pot and finish cooking the pasta with the sauce (i.e. pour the fully drained pasta into the sauce and cook for an additional minute or two and toss with fresh rinsed and shredded basil leaves).

Handwritten recipe on next page.

Contributed by Anthony Brochetelli

Penne ala Vodka

Penne ala Vodka

1 28 oz can of San Marzano Tomatoes
1 cup of heavy cream
½ cup of pecorino romano
½ cup of parmigiano reggiano
½ of an Vidalia Onion
3 cloves of finely chopped garlic
½ teaspoon of crushed red pepper flakes.
Handful of fresh basil leaves
1 cup of wine (optional)
½ can of tomato paste
Penne pasta enough for 4 people.
1 tablespoon of calabrian chili paste
optional (if you prefer spicy)

Cabbage Rolls

INGREDIENTS

1 large head of cabbage
2 lb ground beef
1 to 1 ¼ cups uncooked rice
1 large onion
1 small can sauerkraut
1 tsp garlic powder
2 tsp salt

DIRECTIONS

Parboil cabbage
Mix other ingredients and form into rolls, roll into cabbage leaves.
Layer in pan and cover with Tomato juice.
Place in a 350 degree preheated oven and cook until rice is done (about 1 hour).

NOTES

Contributed by Penny Manahan via Helene Robinson

Cabbage Rolls
1 - Large Head Cabbage
2 lb Ground Beef
1 to 1¼ Cup Rice (uncooked)
1 Large Onion
1 Sm Can Sauer Kraut
1 tsp Garlic Powder   2 tsp Salt.
Par Boil Cabbage

Mix Other Ingr. + form into
Rolls - And Roll into Cabbage
leaves -
Layer in Pan + Cover
with Tomato juice
Cook till Rice is done.
   (About 1 hour)

              PENNY MANAHAN
           COLOMBUS, OH

Bolognese

INGREDIENTS

1 can of San Marzano Tomatoes (35 oz)
1 small tin of tomato paste
1 carrot (finely chopped)
1 onion (finely minced)
1 stalk of celery
½ tsp of fennel seeds (optional)
½ lb ground turkey (for a richer/heavier taste you can go with beef or pork, which tends to be greasier)
½ lb Sweet Italian Chicken Sausage removed from casing
1 glass of dry red wine
1lb of fresh pasta
salt and pepper to taste
Fresh basil leaves (fully rinsed and cleaned)

DIRECTIONS

Saute the soffritto (i.e. finely chopped trio of onion, carrot, and celery) in olive oil until onions are translucent. Add fennel seeds and touch of red pepper flakes. Add tomato paste and cook a few more minutes.

Add ½ lb of ground turkey and ½ lb of ground sausage. After meat is nearly browned, deglaze with cup of wine. Add can of tomatoes and cook for about 1-1 ½ hours on a low flame until sauce is thick enough to stand a spoon up in it without it falling over.

Shred handfuls of basil at end of cooking process and toss directly with pasta, preferably fresh tagliatelle or pappardelle.

Contributed by Anthony Brochetelli

Bolognese Sauce

1 35 oz can of San Marzano tomatoes
1 small can of tomato paste
1 carrot (finely chopped)
1 onion (finely minced)
1 stalk of celery
1/2 teaspoon of fennel seeds
1 lb of ground turkey
1/2 lb of Italian sausage (removed from casing)
1 glass of Dry red wine (Malbec if possible)
1 lb of fresh garlic (preferably from Italy)
salt and pepper to taste

Note: never use cooking wine
if you have the choice! Always
cook with a wine that you would
prefer the taste. Dry wine is better
than sweet for Bolognese.

NOTES

Never use cooking wine if you have the choice! Always cook with a wine that you would prefer the taste. Dry wine is a better choice than sweet for Bolognese.

Mama's Chicken Pie

INGREDIENTS

4 large chicken breasts, cooked and de-boned
2 cups chicken broth
1 can cream of chicken soup
1 cup buttermilk + 1 cup self-rising flour + 1 stick of
butter (melted) mix together.
Peas
Carrots

DIRECTIONS

Butter a 9 x 13 casserole dish. Add chicken, sprinkle peas
and carrots over chicken.
Mix broth with soup and pour over chicken.
Spoon the buttermilk mix over casserole.
Bake at 400 degrees until brown.

NOTES

Contributed by Lib Porter via Helene Robinson

HERE'S WHAT'S COOKING: Mama's Chicken Pie
FROM THE KITCHEN OF: Lib Porter Pickens SC

~ 4 large chicken breasts - cooked
   and deboned.
~ 2 cups chicken broth
~ 1 can cream of chicken soup
~ peas
~ carrots

Butter 9"x13" casserole. Add chicken
to casserole dish. Sprinkle peas
and carrots over chicken. Mix broth
with soup and pour over chicken.
Mix 1 cup buttermilk with 1 cup
self-rising flour and 1 stick of

HERE'S WHAT'S COOKING:
FROM THE KITCHEN OF:

butter (melted). Mix and spoon
over casserole. Bake at 400° until
brown.

163

Chile Rellenos

INGREDIENTS

Small 4 oz can full sliced chilies
(Or 9 fresh parboiled)
1 lb thick-sliced Monterrey Jack cheese
4 eggs separated
½ tsp salt
3 lbs flour
¼ cup evaporated milk

DIRECTIONS

Layer cheese and peppers
Beat eggs whites until stiff
Separately, beat egg yolks, add salt, flour, milk
Fold the two egg mixtures together and pour over
peppers.
Bake for one hour at 225 degrees.
Cover with half of sauce of your choice. Bake ½ hour.

NOTES

Contributed by Linda Larson

Really Fabulous

Chili Relleno — Submitted by Linda Larson

small 4 oz. can full chili stem (or boil fresh (9 fresh)

1 lb. thick slices Monterey cheese

4 eggs — separated

½ tsp salt

3 tbs. flour

¼ cup evaporated milk

—

Layer cheese & peppers.

beat white stiff
"   yolks add salt flour milk
fold 2 egg mixture together
pour over peppers.
bake 1 hr 250

cover with half of sauce
bake ½ hr.

serve with remain sauce

saute 1 dice onion 1 clove garlic
and
2 cups tomato sauce
+ 1 tsp oregano
salt & pepper to taste

Ed's Meatballs

Ingredients

1 lb ground beef
2 handfuls of wet, squeezed french bread
1 clover garlic, minced
½ cup grated Parmesan cheese
2 eggs
pepper
salt
Parsley (lots)

DIRECTIONS

Mix all ingredients together.
Fry until done
Drop meatballs into tomato sauce

NOTES

Contributed by Carla Winter

Ed's Meatballs   2/20/28

1 lb ground beef
2 handfulls of squeezed wet sweet french bread
1 clove garlic minced
1/2 cup grated parmesan cheese
2 eggs
pepper
salt
parseley (lots)
Mix, fry, drop in tomato sauce

Prime Rib

INGREDIENTS

Prime Rib for 2 or 2 ½ in. Sirloin

1 rib of standing rib (2 ½ lb)
1 Tbsp oil
1 small clove
2 large baking potatoes

DIRECTIONS

Ed. Note: Gram Clapp apparently didn't include directions.
Google says to cook your rib roast for a total of 15 minutes per pound. This will result in a medium rare center.

NOTES

Contributed by Gram Clapp via Tricia Clapp

From the Kitchen of: _Gram Clapp_ 7.13.08
Recipe For: _Prime Rib for 2 or 2½_
in. Sirloin   (frozen)

1 rib of standing rib 2½ (lb)
1 T oil
1 sm clove
2 lg baking potatoes
                    1¼ R.

Oven Temperature: _400°_ Time: _1½ M_ Serves: _____
                    1¾R

Moussaka

INGREDIENTS

1 eggplant, slicked thick
8 oz ground turkey
1 cup chopped onion
¼ cup dry red wine
2 Tbsp water
2 Tbsp minced parsley
1 Tbsp tomato paste
1 slice bread, crumbed

1 oz cheese, shredded
¼ tsp cinnamon
1 Tbsp + 1 tsp non-hydrogenated margarine
1 ½ Tbsp flour
Dash nutmeg
½ cup evaporated skim milk
¼ cup water
1 egg, beaten

DIRECTIONS

Sprinkle eggplant with salt and set aside to drain moisture. Brown turkey and onion in skillet. Drain. Add wine, water, parsley, tomato paste, salt and pepper. Simmer until fairly dry. Set aside.

Mix together half of the cheese, half of the bread crumbs and the egg. Stir into the meat mixture with the cinnamon. Set aside.

In a saucepan make a cream sauce with the margarine, flour, nutmeg, milk, water. Stir half of this mixture into the remaining egg and then add this mixture to the sauce. Simmer +/- 2 minutes.

Sprinkle remaining bread crumbs in sprayed casserole. Place a layer of eggplant slices on bottom. Cover with meat mixture. Top with more eggplant. Pour cream sauce over all. Sprinkle with remaining cheese. Bake uncovered about 45 minutes at 350 degrees.

Contributed by Peg Brantley

MOUSSAKA   (Well worth the effort!)

1 eggplant, sliced thick
8 oz ground turkey
1 c chopped onion
¼ c dry red wine
2 T water
2 T minced parsley
1 T tomato paste
1 oz RC bread, crumbed
1 oz cheese, shredded
1 egg, beaten

¼ t. cinnamon
1 T + 1 t RC margarine
1½ T flour
dash nutmeg
½ c evaporated skim milk
¼ c water
1 egg, beaten

4 SERVINGS
2 ¼ P, ¼ M, ½ FA, 2 V,
½ B, 23 C'

Sprinkle eggplant with salt & set aside to drain
moisture. Brown turkey & onion in skillet. Drain.
Add wine, water, parsley, tomato paste, salt & pepper.
Simmer until fairly dry. Set aside.
    Mix together half of the cheese, half of the
bread crumbs & the egg. Stir into the meat
mixture with the cinnamon. Set aside.
    In a saucepan make a cream sauce
w/the margarine, flour, nutmeg, milk & water. Stir
half of this mixture into the remaining egg & then
add this mixture to the sauce. Simmer ± 2 min.
    In a sprayed casserole, sprinkle remaining bread
crumbs. Place a layer of eggplant slices on bottom.
Cover w/meat mixture. Top w/more eggplant. Pour the
cream sauce over all. Sprinkle with remain. cheese.
Bake uncovered at 350° about 45 minutes.

Chipper Tuna Casserole

INGREDIENTS

1 can cream of celery soup
1 can tuna (6 ½ oz drained)
½ to 1 cup of milk
½ cup English peas (drained)
1 cup of cooked noodles
2 ¼ cups crushed potato chips

DIRECTIONS

Mix in a 1 quart casserole the soup, milk, tuna, peas, noodles, and 2 cups of crushed potato chips.
Put ¼ cup of crushed potato chips on the top of mixed casserole.
Bake for 25 minutes at 325 degrees.

NOTES

Contributed by Lib Porter via Helene Robinson

Chipper Tuna Casserole

1 can Cream of Celery Soup
1 can of Tuna (6½ oz.) (drained)
½ to 1 cup of milk
½ cup (drained) English peas
1 cup of cooked noodles
2¼ cups of crushed potato chips

Mix in 1 quart casserole: soup, milk, Tuna, peas, noodles and 2 cups of crushed potato chips. Put ¼ cup of crushed potato chips on the top of mixed casserole. Bake at 325° or 35° for 25 minutes.

LIB PORTER
PICKENS, SC

173

Baked Stuffed Shrimp

INGREDIENTS

12 jumbo shrimp
2 cups coarsely crushed saltine crackers
½ cup grated sharp cheese (I use canned Parmesan)
½ tsp pepper
1 tsp garlic powder
1 cup melted butter

DIRECTIONS

Peel shrimp leaving tail intact. Slit down center, clean, place on cookie sheet or roasting pan.
Mix crackers, cheese, spices, and butter. Place mound of mixture on each.
Bake 15 minutes at 350 degrees (for smaller shrimp adjust time).

NOTES

Sometimes the whole cup of butter is not needed, so start with less.

Contributed by Tricia Clapp

Baked Stuffed Shrimp

12 jumbo shrimp

2 C. coarsely crushed Saltines

1/2 C. grated sharp cheese (I use the canned parmesan)

1/2 Tsp pepper

1 tsp. garlic powder

1 C. melted butter

(over)

Peel shrimp leaving tail intact. Slit down center, clean, place on cookie sheet or roast pan. Place mound of mixture on each. Bake 350° 15 min. (For smaller shrimp adjust time.)

Sometimes the whole cup of butter is not needed so start with less.

Chicken Marsala

INGREDIENTS

Golden Crusted Chicken

2 large chicken breasts
½ tsp cooking salt/kosher salt
½ tsp black pepper
¼ cup all-purpose flour

Marsala Sauce

2 Tbsp extra virgin olive oil
2 Tbsp unsalted butter
2 shallots - small diced
1 garlic finely minced
2 cups white mushrooms sliced
1 cup dry Marsala wine
½ cup chick stock or broth
½ cup heavy cream
¼ tsp cooking salt/kosher salt
1/8 tsp black pepper
1 Tbsp finely chopped parsley

DIRECTIONS

Butterfly chicken breasts to create 4 thin steaks. Cover with plastic wrap and pound until thin. Sprinkle the surface with half the salt, pepper, then flour lightly, rub flour across the surface. Turn and repeat with remaining salt, pepper and flour. Shake excess flour off each piece before cooking.

Contributed by Sara Taylor via Sheila Lowe (her sister)

Cook: Melt half the butter and oil in a large pan over medium-high heat. Once the butter is melted and foamy, add chicken and cook 3-4 minutes until golden and crispy. Turn and cook other side for 2 minutes. Remove to a plate.

Creamy Marsala Sauce

Saute aromatics in the pan, add remaining butter and oil. Once butter is melted, add shallots and garlic. Cook for 1 minute.

Add mushrooms. Cook for 3 minutes, stirring regularly.

Reduce Marsala - add Marsala, turn up heat to high and boil for 3 minutes or until reduced by half.

Thicken sauce - Add chicken stock, cream, salt and pepper. Stir, then lower heat to simmering (not boiling), and simmer for 3-5 minutes until the sauce thickens to a cream consistency (not too thick—it will thicken more). Remove chicken and nestle into sauce. Leave for 30 seconds to reheat.

Remove from stove, sprinkle with parsley and serve over starchy vehicle of your choice (I chose pasta).

Handwritten recipe next pages

Chicken Marsala

Serves 4

Golden crusted chicken
2 large chicken breasts
1/2 tsp cooking salt/kosher salt
1/2 tsp black pepper
1/4 cup all-purpose flour

Marsala Sauce
2 tbsp extra virgin olive oil
2 tbsp unsalted butter
2 shallots - small dice
1 garlic - finely minced
2 cups white mushrooms - sliced
1 cup dry marsala wine
1/2 cup chic[ken]
1/2 cup heav[y]
1/4 tsp cooki[ng]
1/8 tsp blac[k]
1 tbsp fine[ly]

Creamy Marsala Sauce

Sauté aromatics - In the ~~sand~~ pan add remaining butter and oil. Once butter is melted, add shallots and garlic. Cook for 1 minute

Cook mushrooms - Add mushrooms. Cook for 3 minutes, stirring regularly

Reduce marsala - Add marsala, turn up heat to high and boil for 3 minutes or until reduced by half.

Thicken sauce - Add chicken stock, cream, salt and pepper. Stir, then lower heat so its simmering (not boiling rapidly) and simmer for 3-5 minutes until the sauce thickens to a cream consistency (not too thick, will thicken more)

Rewarm chicken - Nestle chicken into sauce and leave for 30 seconds to reheat

<u>Instructions</u>

Butterfly chicken breasts to create 4 thin steaks. Cover with plastic wrap and pound until thin.

Dust - Sprinkle the surface with half the salt, pepper, then flour. Lightly rub flour across the surface, turn and repeat with remaining salt, pepper and flour. Shake excess flour off of each piece before cooking.

Cook - Put half the butter and oil in a large pan over medium high heat. Once the butter is melted and foamy, place chicken in then cook for 3-4 minutes until it's golden and crispy. Turn and cook other side for 2 minutes. Remove onto a platter.

Serve! Take off the stove. Garnish with parsley, serve over starchy vehicle of choice (I chose pasta).

Green Chili Stew

DIRECTIONS

Cut round steak into small cubes and dredge with flour, salt, and pepper. Brown in oil in which garlic has been fried over hot fire.

Add chopped onions and large can of chopped green chilis.

Add 1 lb can tomatoes (too many tomatoes unfavorably affects taste).*

Simmer in covered pan until meat is tender (30-45 minutes).

Thicken if needed by adding more flour or cornstarch.

* I often add chopped fresh bell peppers, and usual season with cayenne, rosemary, oregano, cumin, and coriander (sometimes a blob of Victoria Ranchera Sauce)

NOTES

Contributed by Carla Winter

Green Chili Stew

Cut roundsteak into small cubes & dredge with flour, salt, & pepper. Brown in oil in which garlic has been fried over hot fire. Add chopped onions & large can chopped green chilis. Add 1 lb. can tomatoes (too many tomatoes unfavorable affect taste).*
Simmer in covered pan until meat is done (30-45 min.).
To thicken if needed, add more flour or cornstarch.

* I often add chopped fresh bell peppers, & usually
season with cayenne, rosemary, oregano, cumin, &
coriander (& sometimes a blob of Victoria Ranchera Sauce).

Lib's Roast Pork

INGREDIENTS

4 to 5 lb pork roast
2 cups water
1 cup strong black coffee
½ cup Worcestershire sauce
¼ tsp garlic powder
¼ tsp salt
¼ tsp pepper
¼ tsp ground cloves
¼ tsp ground thyme

DIRECTIONS

Place pork roast in baking pan. Pour 2 cups water in pan.
Mix coffee and Worcestershire sauce over roast. Mix
remaining ingredients and pour over roast. Seal pan with
foil. Bake 1 hour per lb of pork at 325 degrees.

NOTES

Contributed by Lib Porter via Helene Robinson

Lib's Pork Roast

4 to 5 lbs. pork roast
2 cups water
1 cup strong black coffee
½ cup worchestershire sauce
¼ teaspoon garlic powder
¼ t. salt
½ t. pepper
¼ t. cloves (ground)
½ t. thyme (ground)

Place pork roast in baking pan. Pour 2 cups water in pan. Mix coffee + worchestershire sauce over roast. Mix remaining ingredients and pour over roast. Seal pan with foil.
Bake at 325°. Bake 1 hr per lb. of pork roast.

LIB PORTER
PICKENS, SC

Peking Pork Ribs

DIRECTIONS

Pork ribs - 1 catty (approx 1.5 pounds)

Cut pork ribs into small chunks; marinate in light soy sauce, egg and flour.

Heat cooking oil and deep-fry ribs until done. Drain oil.

Fry ginger and spring onion in hot oil; add light soy sauce, tomato sauce, wine, sugar, vinegar, sesame oil, and water. Bring to a boil. Thicken the sauce

(Ed. Note: use cornstarch to thicken);

Add the pork ribs to the sauce and mix well.

NOTES

Note: "catty" is a measurement that equals about 1.33 lbs or 604 g.

Contributed by Mon Ho via Maria Lam (Hong Kong)

Peking Pork Ribs

Ingredients:

Pork ribs   1 catty.

Steps:

① Cut pork ribs into small chunks; marinate the ribs with light soy sauce, egg and flour.

② Heat cooking oil and deep-fry the ribs until done; drain oil.

③ Fry ginger and spring onion in hot oil; add light soy sauce, tomato sauce, wine, sugar, vinegar, sesame oil, and water and bring to the boil; thicken the sauce; add the pork ribs and mix well; serve.

Flank Steak with Whiskey Sauce

INGREDIENTS

¼ cup teriyaki sauce

4 garlic cloves, minced, divided

2 tsp each red wine vinegar and Worcestershire sauce

1/8 tsp hot sauce

15 oz beef flank steak

1 Tbsp and 1 tsp margarine

¼ cup minced onion

1/3 cup plus 2 tsp whiskey

DIRECTIONS

In medium glass or stainless steel bowl combine teriyaki sauce, 1 ½ tsp garlic, and the vinegar, Worcestershire sauce, and hot sauce; add steak and turn several times to coat. Cover with plastic wrap and refrigerate overnight or at least 30 minutes. In small saucepan heat margarine over medium heat until bubbling; add onion and remaining garlic. Saute until translucent.

Discarde marinade, transfer steak to rack in broiling pan, turning once until steak is rare, about 4 minutes on each side. Slice across the grain, top with sauce and garnish with watercress.

4 servings

NOTES

Contributed by Peg Brantley

Flank Steak with Whiskey Sauce

¼ c teriyaki sauce
4 garlic cloves, minced, divided
2 tsp. each red wine vinegar and
  Worcestershire sauce
⅛ tsp. hot sauce
15 oz beef flank steak
1 T. + 1 tsp. margarine
¼ c. minced onion
⅓ c plus 2 tsp. whiskey

In medium glass or stainless-steel bowl
combine teriyaki sauce, 1½ tsp. garlic,
and the vinegar, Worcestershire sauce,
and hot sauce; add steak and turn
several times to coat. Cover with
plastic wrap and refrigerate overnight
or at least 30 minutes.
   In small saucepan heat margarine
over medium heat until bubbly-hot; add
onion + remaining garlic; sauté until

   Transfer steak to rack in
broiling pan, discarding marinade;
broil, turning once, until steak
is rare, about 4 minutes on
each side. Slice steak across
the grain, top with sauce, and
garnish with watercress.

Makes 4 servings.

Hawaiian Chicken

INGREDIENTS

3 lbs chicken wings cut in sections
2 onions, diced
½ cup celery, diced

DIRECTIONS

Brown chicken in oleo or oil, then remove from pot.
Saute onion and celery until soft in same pot as chicken.
Replace chicken in pot.

Cook 2 cups raw rice in 4 cups water.
Add cooked rice to chicken mixture, add salt and pepper
to taste.
Mix 3 ¼ cup chopped parsley. Add 1 can crushed
pineapple.
Correct seasonings (?).
Bake in covered casserole for 1 hour at 350 deg.

NOTES

Contributed by Carla Winter

Hawaiian chicken

3 lbs chicken wings — cut in sections
& Brown in oleo or oil (Remove
from pot after browning
3 onions — diced } Saute til soft
1/2 c celery — diced } in same
fat as chicken

Replace chicken
Cook 2 c raw rice in 4 c water

Add cooked rice to chicken —
veg mixture. Salt & Pepper

Mix thru 1/4 c chopped parsley
Add 1 can crushed pineapple
Correct seasoning.

Bake in covered casserole
in 350° oven for 1 hour.

Linguine

INGREDIENTS

1 lb linguine
¼ cup olive oil
3 to 4 cloves minced garlic
2 medium or 1 large can(s) chopped clams
chopped/diced parsley
½ tsp basil
pepper

DIRECTIONS

Heat oil, add garlic (don't allow to brown), add clam juice, basil. Simmer while pasta is cooking. Add clams, some pepper, parsley, just before mixing with pasta.

Prepare linguine according to package, approximately 10 minutes.

NOTES

Contributed by Carla Winter

LINGUINI

olive oil — ¼ c prox
3 to 4 cloves garlic minced
2 cans chopped clams or
1 Big can
chopped/diced parsley
½ tsp Basil
pepper

1# linguine / cook in
boiling H₂O til Al dente
prox 8 MIN

Heat oil, add
garlic (don't
let brown)
add juice from
clams, basil

simmer above
while pasta is
cooking. Add
clams & some
pepper, and
parsley just
before mixing
with pasta

Chicken Enchiladas

INGREDIENTS

1 stick butter
1 medium onion
1 small can green chilis
3 boneless chicken breasts
1 can cream of mushroom soup
1 can cream of chicken soup
1 pt sour cream
2 cup grated cheddar cheese
1 pkg corn or flour tortillas

DIRECTIONS

Boil chicken, microwave butter, onion and green chilis.
Add cream of chicken soup, stir. Mix sour cream and
cream of mushroom soup. Dice chicken, add to butter
and chilis.
Fry corn tortillas, stuff with chicken mixture. Spread sour
cream mix on top of filled tortillas. Top with cheese.
Bake for 35-40 minutes at 375 degrees.
Or microwave until cheese melts.

Serves 4 (makes 10 enchiladas)

NOTES

Contributed by Peg Brantley

Chicken Enchiladas

1 stick butter
1 med. onion
1 sm. can grn. chilis
3 boneless chicken breasts
1 can cream of mushroom soup
1 can cream of chicken soup
1 pt. sour cream
2 c. grated cheddar cheese
1 pkg corn tortillas
  or flour tortillas

Boil chicken, microwave butter
onion and green chilis. add
cream of ~~mushroom~~ chicken
soup. Stir. Mix sour cream
and cream of mushroom soup.
Dice up chicken add to butter,
grn chilis.
Fry corn tortillas. Stuff
with chicken mix. Spread
sour cream mix on top of
filled tortillas. Top with
cheese.
Bake at 375° for 35-40 min.
or microwave until cheese melts.
  Serves 4. (makes 10 enchiladas)

Accidentally Wonderful Chicken x 2

INGREDIENTS (1)

4 boneless, skinless chicken breasts
1 cup mayonnaise or yogurt
½ cup Parmesan cheese
1 tsp seasoned salt
½ tsp black pepper
1 tsp garlic

DIRECTIONS

Combine mayo, cheese, and seasoning. Spread on top of chicken. Bake 40-45 minutes at 375 degrees.

Cheese Tortellini and Chicken (2)

Cook boneless, skinless chicken breasts with garlic. Cut into bite-sized pieces.
Thoroughly cook tortellini according to package.
Use hummus with sun dried tomatoes as sauce.
Top with Parmesan, Romano **and** Gorgonzola cheeses.

NOTES

Sometimes we just happen upon some great combination of tastes. Hear are two recipes I happened upon, and still use from time to time.

Eat that thang!

Contributed by Linda Larson

2 accidentaly Wonderful Chicken recipes

Sometimes, we just happen upon some great combination of things. Here are two recipes I happened upon, and still use from time to time.

Melt-In-Your-Mouth Chicken (very yummy & tender.)

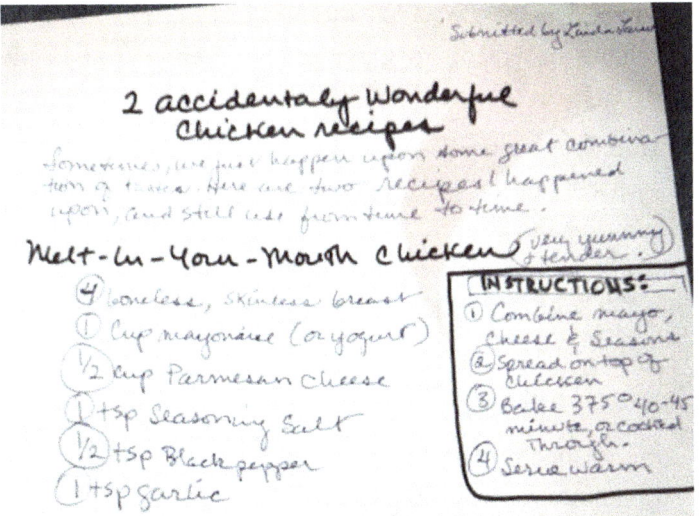

- ④ boneless, skinless breast
- ① cup mayonaise (or yogurt)
- ½ cup Parmesan cheese
- ① tsp Seasoning Salt
- ½ tsp Black pepper
- ① tsp garlic

INSTRUCTIONS:
① Combine mayo, Cheese & Seasons
② Spread on top of chicken
③ Bake 375° 40-45 minute, or cooked Through.
④ Serve warm

Cheese Tortellini + Chicken

- Cook up chicken breast (boneless, skinless) w/garlic
- Cut into bite sized pieces.
- Thoroughly cook Tortellinis
- Use Hummus w/ Sundried tomatoes as "Sauce
- Top w/ Parmesan/Romano and Gorgonzola Cheeses to top.

Eat That Thang!

Meatza Pie & Potato Waffles

INGREDIENTS and DIRECTIONS

1 lb lean ground beef
½ cup milk
1/3 breadcrumbs
½ tsp garlic salt
Combine ingredients together and pat evenly into a 9" pie plate to form the shell.

Spread over center:
½ cup ketchup or tomato sauce
½ tsp oregano
1 can drained mushroom pieces and stems.
Sprinkle with 1 ½ cups shredded cheddar.

Potato Waffles

Cut 4 washed potatoes in half. On flat side, using tip of paring knife, make hash pattern.

In baking pan, spread 1 Tbsp oil. Sprinkle with 1 tsp coarse salt, 1 tsp garlic powder. Place flat side down in baking pan.

Place both dishes into a 400 degree oven and bake for 30 minutes.

Let sit five minutes, then cut Meatza Pie in quarters to serve along with 2 potato halves.

Enjoy!

Contributed by Edda Manley

Meatza Pie + Potato Waffles

1 lb. lean ground beef
1/2 c. milk
1/3 c. breadcrumbs
1/2 tsp. garlic salt

Mix above ingredients together and pat evenly into 9" pie plate to form the shell.

Into centre spread:
  1/2 c. ketchup or tomato sauce
  1/2 tsp. oregano
  1 can drained mushroom pieces + stems

Sprinkle with 1 1/2 c shredded cheddar.

Potato Waffles

4 washed potatoes cut in half
On flat side, using tip of paring knife score to make hashtag pattern.
In baking pan spread 1 tbsp. oil
Sprinkle with 1 tsp. coarse salt
           1 tsp. garlic powder
Place flat side down in baking pan.

Put both dishes into 400° oven for 30 min. Let sit 5 min. then cut Meatza Pie in quarters to serve along with 2 potato halves.

Enjoy!

197

Apricot Chicken with Edible Flourish

INGREDIENTS

10 ripe apricots, halved
2 Tbsp sugar
Pinch cayenne pepper
4 Tbsp extra virgin olive oil
4 large boneless chicken breasts
2 tsp salt
Fresh ground black pepper

DIRECTIONS

Preheat oven to 425 degrees and line baking sheet with parchment.

Place apricot halves on the sheet.

In a small saucepan, cook diced apricots with all but 1 tsp sugar over medium heat until soft and jam-like.

Brush apricots with olive oil and sprinkle with sugar.

Drizzle olive oil in a roasting dish. Add chicken and coat evenly. Season with salt and pepper.

Spoon 1-2 tsp glaze over each chicken breast.

Roast chicken and apricots for 20-30 minutes until chicken reaches 165 degrees. Baste halfway through.

Let rest for 15 minutes. Slice chicken against the grain and service with roasted apricots.

Hope you love it!

Contributed by Lena Rivkin

Apricot Chicken : Baked with Edible Flourish
Lena Rivkin

Ingredients for 4 servings:

10 ripe apricots
2 tablespoons sugar
Pinch cayenne pepper
4 tablespoons extra virgin olive oil
4 large boneless chicken breasts
2 teaspoons salt
Fresh grinds of black pepper

Instructions

1. Preheat oven to 425°F and line baking sheet with parchment
2. Place apricot halves on the sheet
3. In small saucepan, cook diced apricots with all but 1 tsp sugar over medium heat until soft and jam like.
4. Brush apricot halves with olive oil and sprinkle with sugar
5. Drizzle olive oil in a roasting dish, add chicken, and coat evenly. Season with salt and pepper
6. Spoon 1-2 tsp glaze over each chicken breast
7. Roast chicken and apricots for 20-30 minutes, until chicken reaches 165°F. Baste halfway through
8. Let it rest 15 minutes. Slice chicken against the grain and serve with roasted apricots.

Hope you love it!

Hamburger Bacon Rice Casserole

INGREDIENTS

1 lb hamburger
2 cups celery
little onion
½ green pepper
4 slices bacon
1 can tomatoes (30 oz)
1 clove garlic
Little allspice

2 cups cooked rice

DIRECTIONS

Bake ½ hour 350 degrees.

NOTES

Contributed by Jane O'Brien

Mrs. E. O. Lentz   ‡   Redmond, Wash.

1 # hamberger
2 c. Celery
Little onion
½ gr. pepper
4 slices bacon
1 - 303 x can Tomatoes
1 cloves garlic
little allspice

2 cup. cooked rice
Bake ½ hour
350°

Mom's Meatloaf

INGREDIENTS

1 lb good chopped meat
Bread crumbs
1 egg
1 little milk
1 can Campbell's® vegetarian vegetable soup.

DIRECTIONS

Combine all ingredients until well mixed. Form into a loaf and bake for about 1 hour at 350 degrees.

NOTES

Contributed by Kathleen Dickinson

Recipe: meat loaf

From: mom   Makes:

1 lb good chop meat

bread crumbs

1 egg

a little milk

1 can campbells vegeterian

vegetable soup

Combine all till well mixed

form

350° oven

Baked Seafood Packets

INGREDIENTS

1 lb salmon, orange roughy, or other fish filet
2 Tbsp prepared pesto
2 Tbsp plain non-fat yogurt
1 small tomato, thinly sliced
¼ cup shredded carrots
¼ cup chopped green onions
1 Tbsp lemon juice

DIRECTIONS

Preheat oven to 400 degrees. Tear off 4 large pieces of cooking parchment or foil. Divide fish into 4 equal portions; place one portion on each sheet.

In small bowl, combine pesto and yogurt. Layer tomato slices, carrots, green onions, pesto mixture and lemon juice on each piece of foil. Fold foil to create 4 sealed packets. Transfer to baking sheet.

Bake packets 20-25 minutes or until fish flakes easily when lightly pressed with a fork. Remove fish from pockets and serve with vegetables and cooking juices.

NOTES

You could vary amounts and kinds of veggies or do all in one big packet. If you bake potatoes, the fish could go in oven for the last 20-25 minutes and you'd have the whole meal ready—*voila!* The recipe was in an old nutrition action issue (value of seafood!) and I'm going to try it this week!

Contributed by Kim Woodward

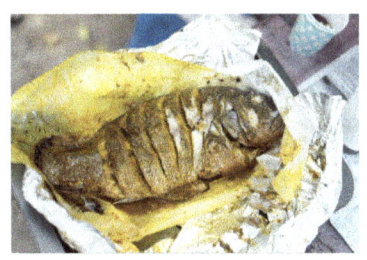

Bakee Seafood Packets

- 1 lb. salmon, orange roughy or other fish fillets
- 2 Tbs. prepared pesto
- 2 Tbs. plain non-fat yogurt
- 1 small tomato, thinly sliced
- 1/4 c. shredded carrots
- 1/4 c. chopped green onions
- 1 Tbs. lemon juice

Preheat oven to 400°. Tear off 4 lg. pcs. of cooking parchment or foil. Divide fish into 4 equal portions; place one portion on each sheet of foil.

In small bowl, combine pesto and yogurt. Layer tomato slices, carrots, green onions, pesto mixture and →

lemon juice on each pc. of foil; fold foil to create 4 sealed packets. Transfer packets to baking sheet.

Bake packets for 20-25 min. or 'til fish flakes easily when lightly pressed with a fork. Remove fish from packets + serve with vegetables and cooking juices.

Serves 4

You could vary amounts + kinds of veggies or do all in one big packet. If you bake potatoes, the fish could go in oven for the last 20-25 min. and you'd have the whole meal ready — VOILA! This recipe was in an old Nutrition Action issue (value of seafood!) and I'm going to try it this week!

MOM

Quiche Lorraine

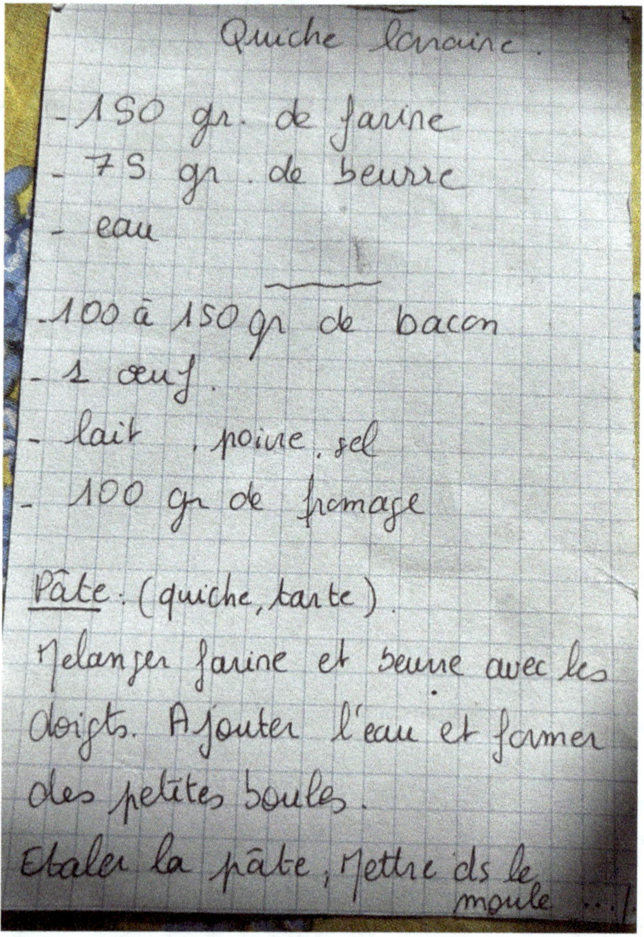

Quiche lorraine.

- 150 gr. de farine
- 75 gr. de beurre
- eau

- 100 à 150 gr de bacon
- 1 œuf.
- lait , poivre, sel
- 100 gr de fromage

<u>Pâte</u> : (quiche, tarte).

Mélanger farine et beurre avec les doigts. Ajouter l'eau et former des petites boules.

Étaler la pâte ; Mettre ds le moule ...!

Contributed by Ruth Holmes

pour la quiche.
tapisser le fond de la pâte avec
les bacons coupés en morceau.
Mélanger lait, œuf, poivre, sel et
fromage rapé.
et Mettre ds le moule sur la pâte.
four chaud. th. 7. pendant 35 mn.
Servir chaud.

   Bon appetit.

Cornish Pasties

INGREDIENTS

Pastry

6 oz plain flour
1 ½ oz margarine
1 ½ oz lard
water
beaten egg + milk

Filling

3 oz ground beef
½ onion, grated
½ potato, grated
seasoning, salt, pepper
water (if necessary)

DIRECTIONS

Rub flour, lard and margarine together and add necessary water. Roll pastry into oval shape (makes 2).

Filling: Mix grated potato and grated onion with mince (ground beef). Add seasoning to filling and spoon onto pastry. Fold onto one side and crimp edges.

Spread with beaten egg and milk. Pierce the top to allow steam to vent. Cook for 35 minutes at 380-480 degrees.

NOTES

Here are two recipes written by me (Sue). They were dictated to me by the cookery teacher at school. I was 13 years old at the time.

Contributed by Susan Ord

Cornish Pasties

pastry
{
6 ozs plain flour
1½ ozs marg
1½ ozs lard
water
}

beaten egg + milk.

<u>Time</u>   30 mins

filling
{
3ozs minced beef
½ onion
✱potato
seasoning, salt, pepper.
water (if necessary)
}

<u>Oven</u>   6 / 380-40

1. Rub flour, lard and marg. together and add necessary water.
2. Mix grated potato and grated onion with the mince
3. Roll pastry into oval shape.
4. Add seasoning to filling and put the filling into pastry.
5. Fold onto one side or up to the top and
6. spread with beaten egg and milk..
7. Cook for 35 mins in oven 350-400.
8. Make 2.

British Sausage Rolls

INGREDIENTS

4 oz plain flour
1 oz lard
1 oz margarine
¼ tsp salt
water to mix
4 oz sausage meat

DIRECTIONS

Pastry

Rub in margarine, lard and flour to breadcrumb-like consistency. Add a little water. Roll pastry into an oblong and roll sausage meat into a line.

Put meat in pastry and glue down with water. Cut into two-inch pieces. Pierce the tops to allow steam to vent. Brush with beaten egg.
Bake for ½ hour at 400 degrees.

Makes approximately 18 sausage rolls

NOTES

Contributed by Susan Ord (age 13), Photo - Chris Meredith

Sausage Rolls.

4 ozs plain flour
1 oz lard
1 oz marg
¼ teaspoon salt
water to mix
4 ozs sausage meat

brush in beaten egg
and milk

Oven 400° 7.
Bake ½ hour.

Method

1 Rub in marg, lard and flour.
2 When like bread crumbs add a little water.
3. Roll pastry into an oblong, and roll meat into a line.
4. Put meat in pastry and glue down with water.
5 Brush with a beaten egg.
6 Cook in oven 400°F for ½ hour
7 Makes approx. 18

Huntington Chicken Casserole

INGREDIENTS

3 cups cooked, diced chicken
2 cups cooked noodles
cooked mushrooms (optional)
2 Tbsp parsley
salt and pepper to taste
chicken gravy (your own or canned)

DIRECTIONS

Mix all ingredients together and pour into a casserole
dish. Top with grated cheese of your choice if desired.
Bake 30 minutes at 350 degrees.

NOTES

Contributed by Sheila Lowe

Huntington Chicken

Make chicken gravy, or use Cannut
heat, stir in 1 C grated cheese
3 C cooked, diced chicken
2 C noodles (mushrooms optional)
2 T Parsley
salt & pepper to taste
bake @ 350° — 30 min

Tamale Pie

INGREDIENTS

1 ½ lbs ground beef fried with onions and garlic until brown.
chili powder to taste (1 ½ Tbsp)
1 can creamed corn
1 can tomatoes
1 can enchilada sauce (hot)
Pinch of oregano
1 can sliced black olives (add last)
1 chopped green pepper

DIRECTIONS

Line baking pan with 1 package of Fritos or cooked corn meal.
Combine ingredients and add to baking pan. Grate cheese on top.
Bake about 1 hour 350 degrees.
Makes approximately 6 servings

NOTES

Contributed by Peg Brantley

Tamale Pie

1½ # ground beef - fry with onions and garlic til brown.

Chili powder to taste (1½ T)

1 cn. creamed corn

1 cn. tomatoes

1 cn. enchilada sauce (hot)

pinch oregano

1 cn. black olives (sliced) (last thing)

1 green pepper, chopped

Line pan with 1 package of fritos or cooked corn meal. Bake 350 degrees about 1 hr. (grated cheese on top).

Makes approx 6 servings

Taco Salad

INGREDIENTS

2 lbs ground beef, browned and cooled
1 can kidney beans, drained
½ head lettuce
Sliced tomato
diced onions
black olives
grated cheese
Doritos and French dressing

DIRECTIONS

Combine all ingredients. Enjoy!

NOTES

Contributed by Peg Brantley

Taco Salad

2 lbs. ground beef
1 can kidney beans
1/2 head lettuce
tomato
onions
black olives
grated cheese
doritos & french dressing

Rolled Chicken Washington

INGREDIENTS

6 skinned and boned whole chicken breasts, pounded flat
Flour for dredging
2 slightly beaten eggs
¾ cup five-day old bread crumbs

Cheese filling

½ cup finely chopped fresh mushrooms, or a 3 oz can of broiled, chopped mushrooms, drained.
2 Tbsp butter
2 Tbsp flour
¼ tsp salt
1 ¼ cup shredded sharp cheddar
½ cup light cream (or canned evaporated milk)
dash cayenne pepper

DIRECTIONS

Saute mushrooms in butter about 5 minutes; blend in flour, stir in cream. Add salt and cayenne, stir until very thick. Stir in cheese. Cook over low heat until cheese melts. Turn mixture into pie plate, cover, chill thoroughly about 1 hour. Cut the firm cheese mixture into 6 equal portions, shape into short sticks and place one on each chicken breast. Lightly coat each breast with oil and flour, form into a roll (secure with a toothpick). Place in shallow baking dish and bake 30-45 minutes at 375 degrees.

NOTES

Ed note: Julie was my roommate after high school. This recipe came from her mother, Evelyn Martin.

Contributed by Juliana Martin via Sheila Lowe

What's cookin' Rolled Chicken Washington Serves

Recipe from the kitchen of Evelyn Martin

½ c. finely chopped fresh
  mushrooms or 1-3 oz.
  can (⅔ c.) broiled, chopped
  mushrooms, drained
2 Tbl. butter 2 Tbl. flour
½ tsp. salt 1¼ c. shredded
             sharp cheese
½ c. light cream (or canned
             milk)
Dash cayenne pepper

6 or 1 boned whole chicken breasts ✻
Flour
2 slightly beaten eggs
¾ c. fine-day bread crumbs

For Cheese Filling: Cook mushrooms in butter about 5 min. Blend in flour, stir in cream. Add salt & cayenne, stir until mixture becomes very thick. Stir in cheese; Cook over low heat until cheese melts. Turn mixture into pie plate. Cover. Chill thoroughly, about 1 hr. Cut the firm cheese mixture into 6-7 equal portions, shape into short sticks.

Anthony's Summer Bruschetta

INGREDIENTS

10 Ripe Plum Tomatoes (stem and seeds removed)
½ teaspoon of Italian Sea Salt
Several tablespoons of unfiltered Taggiasca Olive Oil
(From Liguria)
Several Tablespoons of finely chopped basil leaves
Crostini or Italian toast cut into ten ¼ inch slices (about
4-5 inches in length)
Dried Greek Oregano
A spoonful of red wine vinegar for each slice of toast
Generous handful of fresh basil leaves
Mix ingredients together, spoon onto toast. Serve
immediately.

NOTES

A wonderful dish to serve alongside fresh mozzarella or
burrata in the summer time. Pairs excellently with
Prosecco or grilled fish.

A long French baguette or Pugliese bread from a fine
Italian or French bakery is also excellent.

Contributed by Anthony Brochetelli

Summer Bruschetta

10 ripe plum tomatoes (stems and seeds removed)
1 tsp of finely chopped garlic (fresh or in red onion possible)
1/2 tspoon of Italian sea salt
several tablespoons of unfiltered
   virgin olive oil (to taste)
several tablespoons of finely chopped
   (salt) capers.
castini or (Italian toast cut into
1/4 lb of in each. (10 stems each
   about 4-5 inches)
   in length

dried fresh Oregano
1 spoonful of red wine vinegar for
   each slice of toast
several handful of fresh basil
   leaves.

A wonderful dish to serve
alongside fresh mozzarella in summer
in the summer sun. This
something with Tuscan & grilled
fish.

A very fresh
baguette in Tuscan
and in fine
Italian in finest
Italian, it also excellent.

Spinach Casserole

INGREDIENTS

2 boxes chopped frozen spinach (thawed and well-drained)
1 pkg onion soup mix
1 cup sour cream
1/3 cup dry sherry

DIRECTIONS

Combine all ingredients. Place in casserole dish, spread bread crumbs or dry stuffing mix on top. Dot with margarine or butter.
Bake uncovered 30 minutes at 350 Degrees.

NOTES

Contributed by Jessie McLaughlin via Tricia Clapp

SPINACH CASSEROLE

2 BOXES CHOPPED SPINACH (THAWED AND WELL DRAINED)
1 PKG. ONION SOUP MIX
1 C. SOUR CREAM
1/3 C DRY SHERRY

COMBINE ALL INGREDIENTS. PLACE IN CASSEROLE, PUT BREAD CRUMBS OR DRY STUFFING MIX ON TOP. DOT WITH MARGARINE OR BUTTER. BAKE UNCOVERED 350° 30 MINS.

JESSIE McLAUGHLIN

Green Chile Casserole

INGREDIENTS

2 medium cans diced green chilis
10 oz each: grated jack cheese, cheddar, mozzarella

2 cups milk
2 eggs
½ cup flour

DIRECTIONS

Grease casserole dish with butter and layer.
Combine milk, eggs, flour. Pour and barely cover chilis and cheeses.
Bake 45-60 minutes at 350 degrees. Until golden brown.
Rest for 5-10 minutes before serving.

NOTES

Contributed by Shirley Sargent via Tricia Clapp

3-25-87
Shirley Largent

2 med can wh dice g chiles
1 0 3 each joul cheese
      cheddar } grate
      mozzrella

mix butter casseroles + layer
Combine 2 c milk - 2 eggs 1 1/2 c flour
pour & barely cover.
      Bake at 350 · 45-60
        Golden brown.
let 5-10 min.

Kugel

INGREDIENTS

1 pkg broad noodles, cooked

½ cup brown sugar
½ cup cottage cheese (sour cream)
1 grated apple
cinnamon
plumped up raisins
nuts, orange rind

DIRECTIONS

Combine ingredients above.
Brown ½ cube butter in oven until melted. Add cooked noodles to apple mixture and excess butter, plus 2 beaten eggs. Pour into pan.
Bake 40 minutes at 350 degrees.

NOTES

Contributed by Carla Winter

Kougal   350°   8" pan
1. pkg Bread noodles
½ cup Brown sugar
½ cup cottage cheeze (sour cream)
1 grated apple
cinamon
plump up raisins

nuts
orange
ring

mix

Brwn + cube butter in over until melted -
add cooked noodles to apple mixture +
excess butter + 2 beaten eggs -
  pour into pan
            40 min 350°

229

Cracker Crumb Chestnut Dressing

INGREDIENTS

2 lbs crackers - roll out (crush)
¼ lb butter
8 eggs
2 lbs chestnuts
1 tsp salt
celery leaves cut fine
1 qt milk

DIRECTIONS

Remove hard shell from chestnuts; let the red shell on, cook for 45 minutes to half-hour. Try them. If soft, they are done. Roll the crackers and put in a pan large enough to mix well. Cut butter in small pieces (if you care to use the heart and liver, cut up fine into the rest of the mixture), salt, celery, eggs, milk a little at a time.

Cream from two bottles is good. Clean the chestnuts and cut in pieces, not too big. Add them last when mixing all, not too dry, just nice and smooth. Add milk if needed. Stuff the turkey, sew and roast.

NOTES

In her own words…

"I always soak the turkey a few hours in salt water, then drain off good before you fill it in case you have too much filling. What's left, put by the turkey when it is all done, for a half-hour or in frying pan in the oven. John, I hope you will understand it but you can't go wrong.

You can stuff it at night and put it in the icebox, then in the morning put in the water and in the oven."

Contributed by Mary Horvath Mosko via Sally Mosko

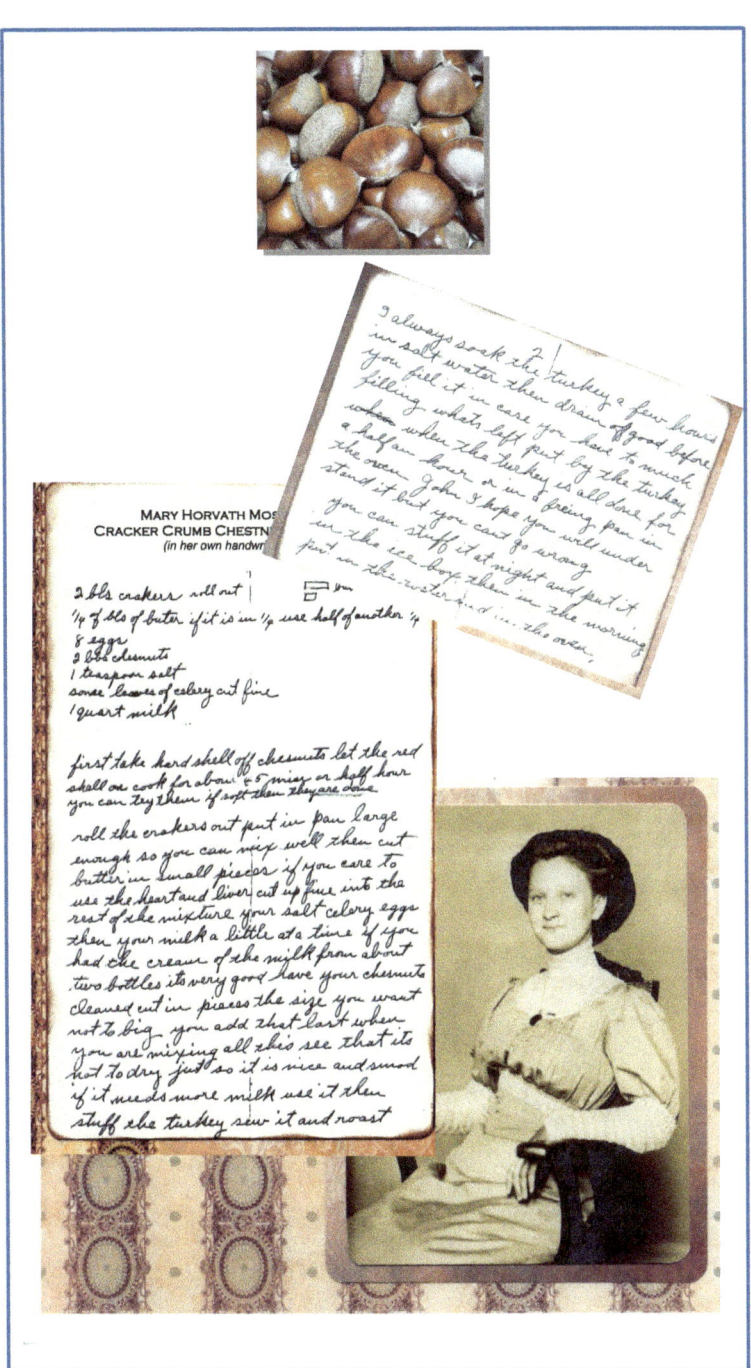

MARY HORVATH MOS...
CRACKER CRUMB CHESTN...
(in her own handwr...)

2 bls crakers roll out
1/4 of bls of buter if it is in 1/p use half of another 1/4
8 eggs
2 bls chesnuts
1 teaspoon salt
sonse leaves of celery cut fine
1 quart milk

first take hard shell off chesnuts let the red
shell on cook for about 15 mier or half hour
you can try them if soft then they are done

roll the crakers out put in pan large
enough so you can mix well then cut
butter in small pieces if you care to
use the heart and liver cut up fine into the
rest of the mixture your salt celery eggs
then your milk a little at a time if you
had the cream of the milk from about
two bottles its very good have your chesnuts
cleaned cut in pieces the size you want
not to big you add that last when
you are mixing all this see that its
not to dry just so it is nice and smod
if it needs more milk use it then
stuff the turkey sew it and roast

2

I always soak the turkey a few hours
in salt water then drain of good before
you fill it in case you have to much
filling whats left put by the turkey
when the turkey is all done for
a half an hour or in a freing pan in
the oven John I hope you will when
stand it but you cant go wrong
you can stuff it at night and put it
in the ice-box then in the morning
put in the water and in the oven.

231

Potato Stuffing

INGREDIENTS

2 cups grated potatoes, drained
½ cup chopped, minced onion
4 Tbsp flour
1 egg
½ tsp salt
pepper

DIRECTIONS

Mix all ingredients and stuff veal (or other meat). Close pocket with skewer or toothpick.

NOTES

Contributed by Carla Winter

– Potato Stuffing
2 c grated potatoes, drained
1/2 c chopped, minced onion
4 T. flour
1 egg
1/2 tsp salt
pepper
Mix all ingreds + stuff veal.
Close pocket with skewer or
tooth pick

Greek Turkey Stuffing

INGREDIENTS

1/8 to ¼ stick butter or ghee
1 lb ground beef
chopped liver from turkey (optional)
2 cloves minced garlic
1 cup chopped celery (strings removed)
1 cup chopped opinion
¼ - 1 cup chopped fresh parsley
1 tsp salt
½ tsp pepper
1 cup long grain raw rice
2 cups water
½ cup currants
½ cup dry white wine
¼ cup pine nuts

DIRECTIONS

Melt butter in large Dutch oven. Brown ground beef (liver). Add vegetables, cook a few additional minutes. Add seasonings and rice. Add water. Cover and cook 20-25 minutes on low flame until rice is tender. While rice cooks, soak currants in wine. When rice is tender, add currants and nuts. Mix well. Enjoy!

Contributed by Betty Rozakis (Greece)

Greek Turkey Stuffing
Betty Rozakis

1/8 - 1/4 stick butter or ghee
1 lb. ground beef
Liver from Turkey chopped (optional)
2 cloves minced garlic
1 cup chopped celery (strings removed)
1 cup chopped onion
1/4 - 1cup chopped fresh parsley
1 teaspoon salt
1/2 teaspoon pepper
1 cup long grain raw rice
2 cups water
1/2 cup currants
1/2 cup dry white wine
1/4 cup pine nuts

Melt butter in large Dutch oven. Brown ground beef (liver) Add vegetables - cook a few additional minutes. Add seasonings & rice. Add water. Cover & cook 20-25 minutes on low flame until rice is tender. While rice cooks, soak currants in wine. When rice is tender, add currants & nuts Mix well—   Enjoy!

Too Busy to Cook

INGREDIENTS

2-3 Tbsp margarine or butter
1 tsp salt
1 clove garlic
1 tsp oregano leaves, crumbled
¼ cup chopped onion
3 medium tomatoes cut ¼" disks
2 pkg (7 oz) frozen snow peas (thawed)
1 can water chestnuts (sliced, drained) 8 oz
1 Tbs soy sauce

DIRECTIONS

Melt butter and garlic in large skilled on medium. Add onion and saute until crisp and tender, about 1 minute. Blend in remaining ingredients (except tomato), and cook constantly, 2-3 minutes. Stir in tomatoes and cook until heated through, about 2-3 minutes.
Serve hot.

Bon Appetit

NOTES

Contributed by Mae Battles via Tricia Clapp

Thai Battes
June 1987

2-3 lbs marg or butter   1 tsp salt
1 clove garlic   1 tsp oregano leaves (crumbled)
1/4 c. ch. onion   3 med tom cut 1/4 dice
2 7 oz pkg frozen
snow peas (thawed)
1 8 oz can water chestnuts
(sliced drained)
1 tb soy sauce   Too Busy to Cook
                          Bon Appétit

Melt butter & garlic in lg skillet over med heat. Add onion & sauté until crisp tender about 1 min. Blend in remaining ingredients (except tom) & cook constantly 2-3 min. Stir in tom & cook until heated through, about 2-3 minutes. Serve hot.

Quesadillas

Ingredients

1 cup cottage cheese
2 eggs
½ cup dried currants
½ cup sugar
1/8 tsp salt

DIRECTIONS

Mash cottage cheese, add well-beaten eggs, salt, sugar and cinnamon.

Roll phyllo dough pastry into very thin sheets and cut into uniform 4-inch squares. Place 1 Tbsp cheese mixture on half of each square. Moisten edges, fold over other half, making a triangle. Press edges together and prick with a fork.

Brush with milk, sprinkle with sugar and bake in a moderate oven for approximately 20 minutes (Ed. Note: 350 deg.?) until brown.

NOTES

Contributed by Peg Brantley

Quesadillas

1 cup cottage cheese
2 eggs
1/2 cup dried currants
1/2 cp. sugar
1/8 tsp. salt

Mash cottage cheese... add well beaten eggs, salt, sugar and cinnamon.

Roll pastry into very thin sheets and cut into uniform 4-inch squares. Place 1 tbs. cheese mixture on half of each square. Moisten edges, fold over other half making a triangle. Press edges together and prick with a fork.

Brush with milk... Sprinkle with sugar & bake in moderate oven until brown... approximately 20 min.

Peg's Potato Salad

INGREDIENTS

7 medium potatoes, boiled and chopped
4-5 boiled eggs, chopped
1 cup mayonnaise (Miracle Whip)
2-3 tsp mustard
¼ cup sugar
salt and pepper to taste
1 Tbsp milk
sweet pickles
1 onion, chopped
radishes (optional), sliced

DIRECTIONS

Mix all ingredients together and chill for at least a half-hour before serving.

NOTES

Contributed by Peg Brantley

Potato Salad
1 c Mayonnaise (Miracle Whip)
2-3 t. mustard
1/4 c sugar
Salt + pepper to taste
1T milk
Sweet pickles
7 med. potatoes
4-5 eggs
1 onion
radishes (opt.)

Cornbread Souffle

INGREDIENTS

1 can creamed corn
1 can regular corn, drained
8 oz sour cream or nonfat yogurt
1 box Jiffy baking mix
2 eggs beaten
1 stick melted butter

DIRECTIONS

Mix all ingredients in casserole dish. Bake 1 hour or until browned at 350 degrees.
Let set 5 minutes before serving.

NOTES

Contributed by Kathleen Dickinson

Recipe: Corn bread souffle

From: _____ Makes: _____

1 can creamed corn

1 can reg corn drained

8 oz sour cream or nonfat
                              yogurt

1 box Jiffy mix

2 Eggs beaten

1 stick butter melted

mix all in casserole dish
put in oven 350° 1 hour
or when browned

let set 5 minutes before
                        serving

Barbara's Polenta Ole

INGREDIENTS

1 lb ground turkey
1 16 oz jar of salsa
2 cups Mexican shredded cheese
1 tube pre-coked polenta (18 oz)

DIRECTIONS

Preheat oven to 350 degrees
Grease 8 x 8 pan with vegetable spray
Brown turkey until no longer pink.
Add salsa to turkey.
Add about ¼ cup water to turkey mixture.
Cook turkey mix for 20 minutes; add water if needed.
Slice polenta in half; slice each half into ¼" slices.
Place half of polenta slices in bottom of prepared pan.
Sprinkle polenta with ¼ cup of cheese.
Spread cooked turkey mix on top of polenta.
Spread one cup of cheese on top.
Layer remaining polenta slices on top of cheese and top with remaining cheese.
Cover with foil and bake 25-30 minutes at 350 degrees.

NOTES

Contributed by Barbara Donato

Barbara's Polenta Olé

Ingredients:

 1 lb ground turkey
 1 16oz jar of salsa
 2 cups Mexican Shredded cheese
 1 tube pre-cooked Polenta (18 oz)

Directions:

Preheat oven to 350°
Spray 8" x 8" pan with vegetable spray
Brown turkey until no longer pink.
Add salsa to turkey
Add about ¼ cup water to turkey mixture
Cook turkey mix for 20 minutes; add more water if needed
Slice polenta in half; slice each half into ¼" slices
Place half of polenta slices in bottom of prepared pan
Sprinkle polenta with ¼ cup of cheese
Spread cooked turkey mix on top of polenta
Put one cup of cheese on top
Put remaining polenta slices on top of cheese
Top polenta with remaining cheese
Cover with foil and bake for 25-30 minutes

Mom's Macaroni and Cheese

INGREDIENTS

1 cup milk
1 lb Velveeta cheese, melted with butter.
Do not boil above.
Add Lea & Perrins sauce.

DIRECTIONS

Make macaroni as package directs.
Mix macaroni and sauce in a casserole dish, sprinkle
Parmesan cheese on top.
Bake at 350 degrees until top browns.

NOTES

Contributed by Kathleen Dickinson

Recipe: Macaroni & cheese

From: Mom   Makes:

1 cup milk

1 lb velvetta melted w/ butter

do not boil above

add lea + perrins sauce

make macaroni as package directs

mix macaroni & sauce in

casserole dish put parmesan

cheese on top

350° oven until top browns

Chawanmushi Japanese Steamed Egg Custard

INGREDIENTS

2 large eggs
1 tsp Dashi stock powder
1 tsp Mirin
1 tsp Light soy sauce
1/8 tsp salt
approx 1 ¼ cups water
42 g Kamaboko (Japanese fish cake)
4 shrimp

DIRECTIONS

Mix Dashi (Japanese stock) stock powder, water. Add
Mirin, soy sauce, salt.
Mix the egg well (not too many bubbles).
Add into Dashi mixture.
—-
For Kamaboko (Japanese fish cake), cut into thin slices.
For shrimp, remove the shell, marinate with sake.
Add shrimp and Kamaboko into bottom of cup.
See illustrated directions on facing page.

NOTES

Contributed by Maria Lam (Hong Kong)

Chawan mushi : Japanese Steamed Egg Custard

<Ingredients>

(a) 2 large Eggs

(b) Dashi stock powder   1 Teaspoon

(c) Mirin   1 teaspoon

(d) light soy sauce   1 teaspoon

(e) Salt   1/8 Teaspoon

(f) water   280 cc

(g) Kamaboko (Japanese fish cake)   42g

(h) Shrimp   4

Steps

(1)   (1) Dashi stock powder 1 teaspoon + 280cc water ⇒ mix it first

     (2) Add 1 teaspoon Mirin + 1 teaspoon light soy sauce + 1/8 teaspoon Salt

(2) 2 Egg   mix the egg, mix it well but try not to create too much bubbles

(3) Add (1) into (2) ⇒ mix it together

(4) For Kamaboko, cut into thin slice

For Shrimp, remove the shell, marinate shrimp with sake

(5) Add shrimp + Kamaboko into the bottom of the cup

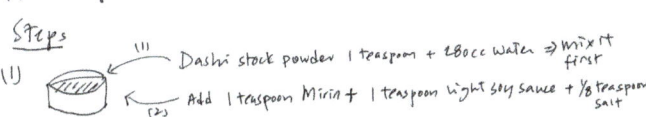

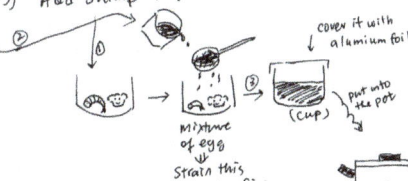

cover it with aluminium foil

put into the pot

(cup)

Mixture of egg
⇩
Strain this through a fine sieve into a bowl

⇒ Add water into the pot that it comes to about halfway up the cup

⇒ Start medium high heat, once water is boiling, put in the cup, close the lid and turn to low heat to cook for further 15 minutes. It's done then

Mom's Mexican Macaroni Con Chili

INGREDIENTS

2 cups macaroni
2 cups tomato sauce
1 onion, chopped
½ cup grated cheese
1 ½ tsp salt
2 Tbsp hot chili sauce

DIRECTIONS

Brown onion in fat. Mix all ingredients with macaroni.
Pour in greased baking dish. Cover with grated cheese.
Bake 30 minutes at 350 degrees.

NOTES

Contributed by Tricia Clapp

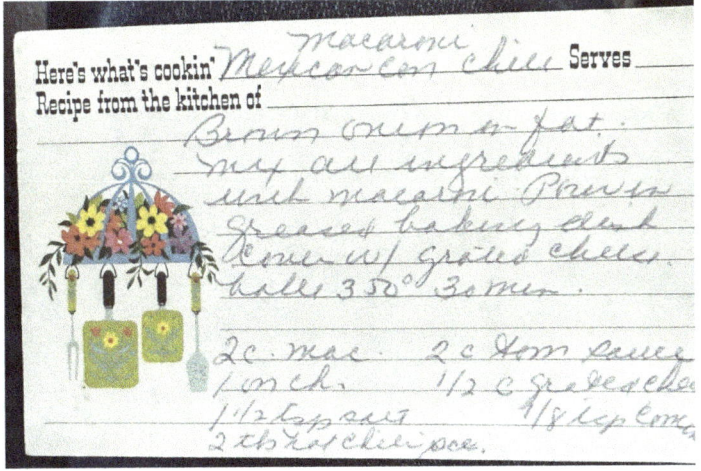

Here's what's cookin' **Macaroni Mexican con chili** Serves _____
Recipe from the kitchen of _____

Brown onion in fat.
mix all ingredients
with macaroni. Pour in
greased baking dish
cover w/ grated cheese.
bake 350° 30 min.

2 c. mac.   2 c tom sauce
1 on ch.   1/2 c grated chee
1 1/2 tsp salt   1/8 tsp corn
2 tb hot chili pce.

251

Jens' Favorite Mushroom Soup

DIRECTIONS

1 kg (approx. 2 lbs) of good, handpicked forest mushrooms (or ½ kg dried and re-hydrated). Saute in butter, and then blend them.

Also blend a finely chopped large onion, a lot of garlic, a large cooked potato, one red bell pepper and a little chile, thyme, and rosemary, etc. (turmeric!).

Cook all for an hour in one liter of water and add salt, pepper, and what you like.

After boiling, add ½ liter or more of whipping cream and a lump of butter. If you have stock from a meat dish from last week, it should definitely go into the soup.

Let the soup rest in the refrigerator and reheat the next day. Then season to taste with sherry or Madeira.

NOTES

Contributed by Jens Windeleff (Denmark)

My favourite mushroom soup: (4-5 people)
1 kg of good, hand picked forest mushrooms
(or 1/2 kg dried and rehydrated), sauté them
in butter, and then blend them. Also blend a
finely chopped large onion, a lot of garlic, a
large cooked potato, one red bell pepper, and
a little chili, thyme, and rosemary, etc.
(turmeric!). Cook it all for an hour in one
liter of water and add spices (salt, pepper)
and what you like. After boiling, add 1/2 liter
or more of whipping cream and a lump of
butter if you have a stock from a meat dish
from last week, it should definitely go into the
soup. Let the soup rest in the refrigerator and
reheat the next day, then season to taste with
sherry or Madeira.
                        Jens W.

255

Turkish Lentil Soup

INGREDIENTS

2 cups washed red lentils
1 carrot
1 potato
1 onion
1 Tbsp tomato paste
2-3 Tbsp olive oil
5-6 cups broth or water
spices: pepper, dried mint, salt, (cumin, dried ginger optional)
1 lemon

DIRECTIONS

Heat the olive oil in a large pot on medium heat. Add the chopped carrots and tomatoes, and tomato paste. Stir for a couple of minutes until onions are soft.

Add the broth or water and lentils, then add all the spices and stir. Add more water or broth if needed.

Cover the soup and cook on low heat for 15-20 minutes until lentils are soft.

Blend the soup using an immersion blender until smooth. Serve with some mint and a little lemon juice. *Afiyet olsun!* ("Enjoy your meal")

NOTES

Ed. note (Sheila): Tuba, my beautiful daughter-in-law, is the mother of my only granddaughter.

Contributed by Tuba Lowe

Turkish Lentil soup

2 Cups washed red lentils
1 carrot
1 potatoe
1 onion
1 tablespoon tomato paste
2-3 tablespoon olive oil
5-6 cups broth or water
spices: pepper, d
(cumin,

1 lemon

Heat the olive oil in a large pot
on medium heat. Add the chopped carrots
and potatoes and tomato paste. Stir
for couple minutes until onions are soft.

Add the broth or water and lentils,
then add all the spices and stir.
Add more water or broth if needed.

Cook the soup until lentils are soft
on low heat for 15-20 minutes with lid.
Blend the soup with an immersion blender
until smooth.

Serve the soup with some mint and
a little bit of lemon juice.
Afiyet olsun!

Cauliflower Mushroom Soup

DIRECTIONS

1 head cauliflower

1 cup shiitake mushrooms

1 cup any other kind of mushrooms

2 small-medium yellow or green squash

1 bunch parsley

1 cup okra and/or green beans (optional)

1 large onion, preferably Vidalia

3 large carrots

1 red pepper

half and half (optional) ½ cup per large soup bowl

2 tsp ground black pepper or peppercorns

2 tsp ground mustard or mustard seeds

1 ½ tsp za'atar or thyme (optional)

4 bay leaves

2 tsp tarragon (optional)

1 tsp ground cayenne pepper (optional)

1 head of garlic (not from China, optional)

Chop all ingredients, set aside parsley leaves from stems

Add all to boiling water except parsley leaves. Simmer for 1 ½ - 2 hours until tender. Add parley leaves at end, let cool. Blend in blender, stir in half and half if desired. Serve with bread

NOTES

The beauty of this recipe is that so many of the ingredients can be added or not, according to taste preferences, food sensitivities and/or availability. For example, not everyone wants that much garlic, but it's important that the garlic NOT come from China. And many people prefer non dairy; the soup works well with or without it.

Contributed by Debbie Berk

Cauliflower Mushroom Soup

Ingredients:

1 head of cauliflower
1 cup shiitake mushrooms
1 cup any other kind of mushrooms
2 small to medium squash (yellow or green)
1 bunch of parsley
1 cup okra or green beans (optional)
1 large onion, preferably Vidalia
3 large carrots
1 red pepper
half & half (optional) ½ cup per large soup bowl
2 teaspoons ground black pepper or peppercorns
2 teaspoons ground mustard or mustard seeds
1½ tsp za'atar or thyme (optional)
2 tsp cumin (optional)
4 bay leaves
2 tsp. tarragon (optional)
1 tsp ground cayenne pepper (optional)
1 head of garlic (not from China, optional)

Chop all ingredients, setting aside parsley leaves from
stems. Add all ingredients to boiling water (except for
parsley leaves). Simmer for 1½ to 2 hours, until all
veggies are tender. Add parsley leaves at end & let
cool for 20 minutes.
Add to blender & blend. Pour into soup bowl
& stir in half & half if desired.
Serve with bread or crackers if desired. Enjoy!

Borscht

INGREDIENTS

1 ¼ lbs beets
1 carrot
1 small onion
4 oz cabbage
2 oz tomatoes
1 oz butter
1 Tbsp vinegar
1 bay leaf
½ Tbsp sugar
salt to taste
¼ pint cream
2 pints water
meat stock

DIRECTIONS

Cook beets; skin and shred finely. Put 4 oz aside to give borscht the color at the end of cooking. Peel carrot and onion, cut into thin strips. Skin tomatoes and chop. Put these ingredients into a pan, pour in enough meat stock to cover, add butter, cover and simmer 20 minutes. Add finely shredded cabbage, bay leaf, oregano, sugar, salt, pepper, and rest of stock. Mix well. Cover and simmer for 20 more minutes. Bring reserved beets to a boil with a cup of stock and 1 Tbsp vinegar. Simmer for a few minutes, strain and add to the borscht. Add the cream as you serve.

Contributed by Christina Strang (England)

BORSCH

1¼ lb   beetroot
1 carrot
1 small onion
4oz cabbage
2oz tomatoes
1 dessert spoon butter
1 tlbspn vinegar
1 bay leaf
½ tbspn sugar
salt to taste
¼ pint cream
2 pints water.

Cook beetroot; skin & shred finely
Put 4oz aside to give borsch the colour at end of
cooking. Peel carrot ronion & cut into thin strips,
skin tomatoes & chop. Put all these prepared
ingredients into a pan, pour in enough meat stock to
cover, add butter, ~~cove~~ cover & simmer for 20 minutes.
Add finely shredded cabbage, bay leaf, vinegar &
~~sige~~ sugar & salt, pepper & rest of stock. Mix well &
cover & simmer for a further 20 minutes. Take the
reserved beetroot, bring to boil with a cup of stock
& 1 tbspn vinegar. Simmer for a few minutes, strain
& add to the borsch. Add the cream as you serve.

Lucynas' Pumpkin Soup

INGREDIENTS

4 ½ cups roasted pumpkin flesh
olive oil
1 onion chopped
garlic, ginger, curry spices (or cinnamon, nutmeg, allspice)
begetable of chicken broth
coconut milk or cream
vinegar (for finishing touch)
salt and/or pepper to taste

DIRECTIONS

Cut pumpkin in half, scoop out seeds, rub with olive oil, salt and pepper. Roast cut side down 40-60 minutes at 390 degrees until soft. Peel skin and measure out flesh.
In a large pot, saute chopped onions until soft. Add spices, garlic and ginger; cook briefly.
Add pumpkin flesh, broth, coconut milk or cream. Simmer for about 20 minutes. Remove from heat, add vinegar and blend until smooth.
Season to taste, serve warm, optionally garnished with toasted pumpkin seeds, or cream drizzle.

NOTES

This recipe is comforting and can be adjusted with spices and toppings to your liking.

Contributed by Lucyna Baca-Lonn (Poland)

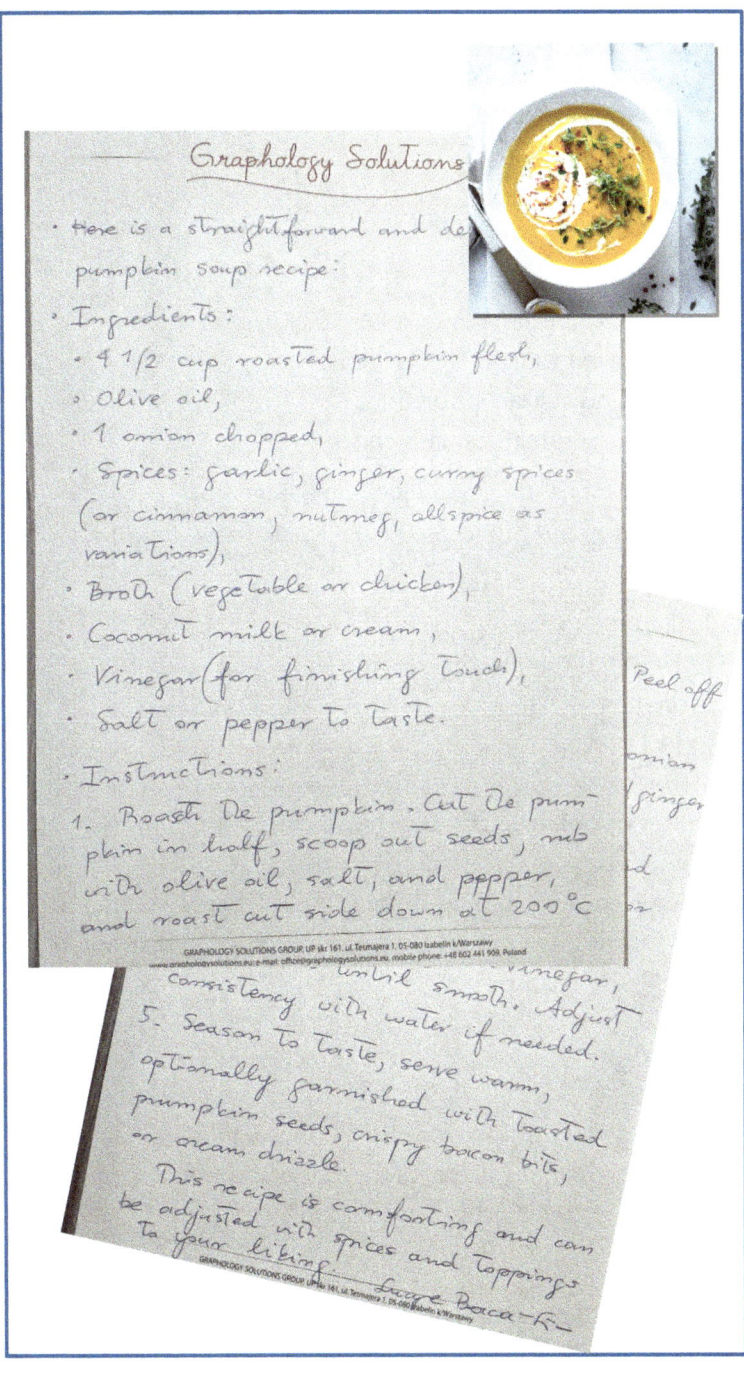

Graphology Solutions

- Here is a straightforward and de[licious]
  pumpkin soup recipe:

- Ingredients:
  - 4 1/2 cup roasted pumpkin flesh,
  - Olive oil,
  - 1 onion chopped,
  - Spices: garlic, ginger, curry spices
    (or cinnamon, nutmeg, allspice as
    variations),
  - Broth (vegetable or chicken),
  - Coconut milk or cream,
  - Vinegar (for finishing touch),
  - Salt or pepper to taste.

- Instructions:
  1. Roast the pumpkin. Cut the pum-
     pkin in half, scoop out seeds, rub
     with olive oil, salt, and pepper,
     and roast cut side down at 200°C

Peel off

onion
ginger

until smooth. Adjust
consistency with water if needed.
5. Season to taste, serve warm,
optionally garnished with toasted
pumpkin seeds, crispy bacon bits,
or cream drizzle.
   This recipe is comforting and can
be adjusted with spices and toppings
to your liking. — Laure Bosca F—

GRAPHOLOGY SOLUTIONS GROUP, UP skr 161, ul. Teunajera 1, 05-080 Izabelin k/Warszawy
www.graphologysolutions.eu e-mail: office@graphologysolutions.eu, mobile phone +48 602 441 908, Poland

GRAPHOLOGY SOLUTIONS GROUP, UP skr 161, ul. Teunajera 1, 05-080 Izabelin k/Warszawy

Taco Soup

INGREDIENTS

2 cans corn
1 can black beans
1 can pinto beans
2 cans diced tomatoes
carrots and celery optional
1 can Rotel tomatoes with chiles

Combine all above ingredients in a large pot.

Brown 1 lb ground beef
1 pkg taco seasoning
1 pkg ranch dressing
½ chopped onion
garlic to taste
½ bell pepper

Add water of half chicken/half beef broth to make 'soupy.'
Bring to near boil, then simmer on low for 30-45 minutes.
Serve with tortilla chips on top, sour cream, Mexican cheese and cilantro.

NOTES

This is a great recipe from my "bonus daughter" and her wife, Heather and Petra. They are both talented women who enjoy making this for their kids.

Contributed by Linda Larson

Submitted by
Linda Larson

This is a great recipe from my "Bonus daughter" and her wife,
Heather & Petra. They are both Talented women & enjoy
making them for their kids!

TACO SOUP

2 cans corn
1 can black Beans
1 can pinto Beans
2 can diced tomatoes
    (carrots & celery can be added too)
1 can rotel tomatoes w/chiles
- Combine all above into a large pot.

- Brown 1 lb ground beef
  1 pkg taco seasoning
  1 pkg Ranch dressing
  1/2 chopped onion
  garlic to taste
  1/2 bell pepper
- add water or half Chicken, half Beef Broth
    "To make Soupy"
- Bring to near boil, then simmer for 30-45 min
                on low.
  - Serve w/ Tortilla chips on top, Sour cream,
    Mexican cheese & cilantro

265

Salmon Sauce

INGREDIENTS

¼ cup fresh cilantro or parsley
3 Tbsp lime juice
4 tsp olive oil
1 minced shallot
1 minced jalapeno
1 minced garlic clove
½ tsp sugar

DIRECTIONS

Whisk and pour over finished salmon

———————————————————

parsley
lemon juice
coconut oil
onion
chili pepper flakes
stevia
garlic

NOTES

Contributed by Peg Brantley

Salmon Sauce
¼ c fresh cilantro or parsley
3 T lime juice
4 t olive oil
1 minced shallot
1 minced jalapeño
1 minced garlic clove
½ t. sugar

Whisk & pour
over finished
Salmon.

Parsley
lemon juice
coconut oil
onion
chili pepper
flakes
stevia
garlic

Physicians WEIGHT LOSS Centers®
Highlands Ranch

Recipe of the Week - Happy Wednesday!

tip of the day
ADD COLOR TO YOUR LIFE

We eat with our eyes first, so make your
look delicious!

Linda's Pumpkin Soup

INGREDIENTS

1 large onion chopped

3 Tbsp butter

½ tsp ground ginger (or more)

½ tsp ground nutmeg

1 large can (29 oz) pumpkin

1 large can (49.5 oz) chicken broth

Salt and pepper

1/3 cup sherry

2-3 cups half and half

DIRECTIONS

Saute onion in butter 15-20 minutes. Add ginger and nutmeg. Puree mixture or just leave chunks.

Return onion to pot, add pumpkin broth (but not all, in case you need less). Salt, pepper, sherry.

Stir and blend 15 minutes. Add half and half.

NOTES

This is comfort food at its best.

Contributed by Linda Larson

This is Comfort food
at its best!

Submitted by
Linda Turin

Pumpkin Soup

1 Lg onion chopped

3 TBLS butter

1/2 tsp ground ginger (or more)
1/2 tsp ground nutmeg

1 Large can (29 oz) pumpkin
1 Large can (49.5 oz) Chicken broth
Salt /pepper
1/3 cup sherry
2 - 3 cups half & half

Saute onion in butter 15 - 20 minutes
add ginger & nutmeg. (Puree mixture
or just leave Chunder

Return Onion to pot, add pumpkin,
broth (but NOT all - incase you
need less). Salt /pepper & sherry
Stir & blend 15 minites add half & half

269

Vegetable Beef Soup

INGREDIENTS

1 lb lean ground beef (brown and drain)
1 cup diced potatoes
1 cup corn
1 cup peas
1 cup lima beans
1 small onion, celery, bell pepper
Tomatoes
Okra

DIRECTIONS

Cook vegetables in 1 quart water. Season with salt and pepper. Add browned ground beef.
Let simmer one hour.
Option: add 1 tsp sugar

NOTES

Contributed by Lib Porter via Helene Robinson

HERE'S WHAT'S COOKING: Vegetable Beef Soup
FROM THE KITCHEN OF: LIB PORTER PICKENS, SC

1 lb. lean ground beef (brown & drain)
Each 1 C. Diced potatoes, corn, peas, lima
1 small onion, celery, peppers. Cook in
1 quart water. Add tomatoes & okra.
Season with salt & pepper. Add brown
ground beef. Let simmer 1 hour
optional t. sugar.

Judy's Loopy Soup

DIRECTIONS

Use a big pot or pressure cooker.
Add the following:
3-5 lbs of any fish you like
Cut fillets into pieces
Cut whole fish in hunks
¼ tsp salt - adjust to taste.
10 lemongrass leaves tied in a loop.
4 sprigs fresh rosemary or 1 tsp dried rosemary in cheesecloth
Add boiling water to cover.
Simmer or pressure cook for 2 hours.
Let cool.
Remove lemongrass and rosemary.
Place fish pieces in bowls and ladle soup on top.
Optional: add cooked rice or noodles.
Serves 8

NOTES

I made up this recipe and call it Loopy Soup. I chose the name Loopy because the recipe requires lemon grass that you tie up in a loop. I have a lemon grass bush but you can buy it in the fresh herbs section of grocery stores. The lemongrass combined with fresh rosemary is surprisingly delicate and delicious.

Contributed by Judy Kaplan

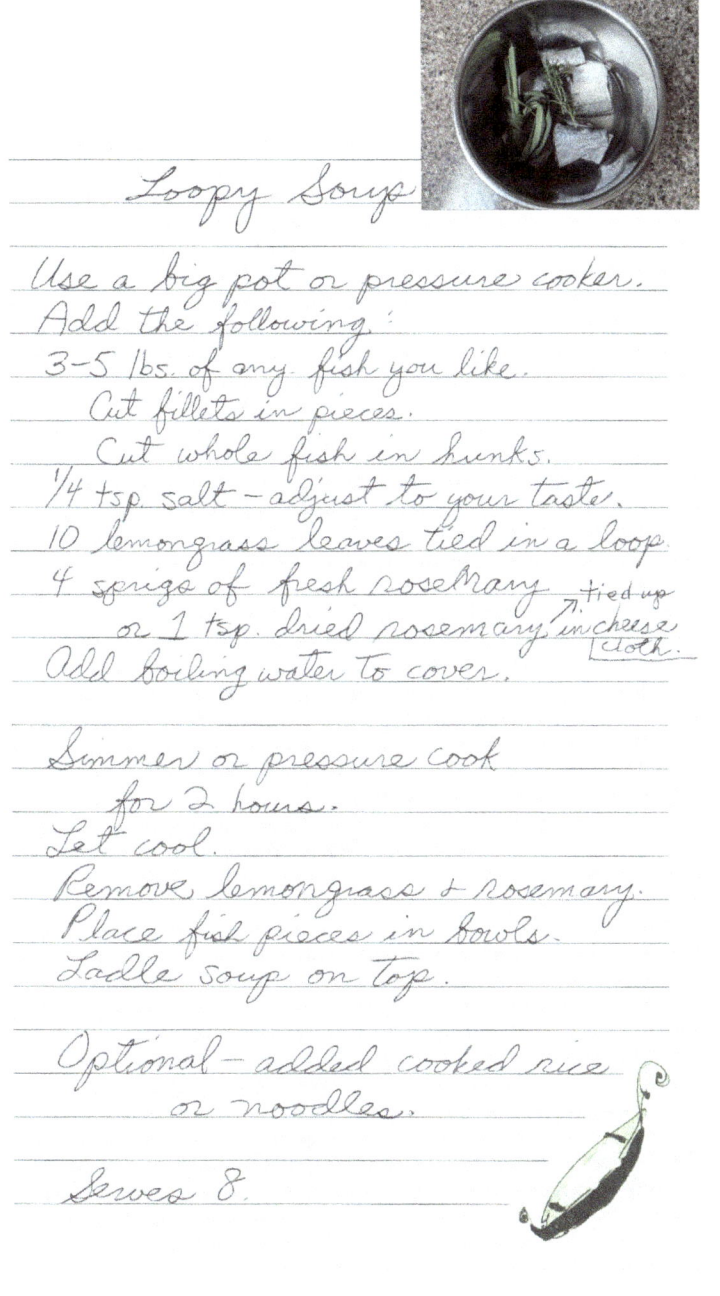

Loopy Soup

Use a big pot or pressure cooker.
Add the following:
3-5 lbs. of any fish you like.
    Cut fillets in pieces.
    Cut whole fish in hunks.
1/4 tsp. salt — adjust to your taste.
10 lemongrass leaves tied in a loop.
4 sprigs of fresh rosemary tied up
    or 1 tsp. dried rosemary in cheese
                              cloth.
Add boiling water to cover.

Simmer or pressure cook
    for 2 hours.
Let cool.
Remove lemongrass & rosemary.
Place fish pieces in bowls.
Ladle soup on top.

Optional — added cooked rice
    or noodles.

Serves 8.

Bountiful Bean Soup

DIRECTIONS

Sort beans and wash thoroughly in water (raw agricultural products may contain foreign materials).

Place beans in kettle, cover with water and soak overnight (add 2 tsp salt if desired).

Drain beans and rinse, add 2-3 quarts of water and 1 lb fresh or smoked ham hock, an onion, and a can of tomatoes or tomato juice. Bring to a boil, lower heat and simmer for 3 hours. Add herb packet (Ed. Note: herbs of your choice or see Notes) to contents and simmer another 20 minutes.

Services 6 to 8. Freezes well. Service with herb bread and salad.

NOTES

Ed. Note: the herb packet might include any or all of the following:
chili powder, cumin, oregano
garlic (dried/minced or powder)
onion (often dried flakes or powder)
black pepper
thyme, bay leaf (one or two whole leaves)
summer savory (less common in all blends, but a traditional bean herb)
paprika, celery seeds, ginger

Contributed by Ruth Holmes

Bountiful Bean Soup

"Beautiful soup! Who cares for fish or game or any other dish? Who would not give all else for two pennysworth only of beautiful soup?" Alice in Wonderland Lewis Carroll

Sort beans, raw agricultural products may contain foreign material, and wash thoroughly in water. Place beans in kettle, cover with water and soak overnight (add 2t. salt if desired) Drain beans and rinse, add 2-3 qts. of water and 1 lb. fresh or smoked ham hock, an onion, and a can of tomatoes or tomato juice. Bring to a boil, simmer for 3 hrs. add herb packet contents and simmer another 20 min. Serves 6 to 8 - Freezes Well - Serve with herb bread & salad.

FRAGRANT HILL FARM
CLARKSTON COUNTRY STORE
21 N. MAIN , CLARKSTON, MI. 48016

Egg Drop Soup

DIRECTIONS

3 cups chicken bouillon (2 cubes)

Add 1 ½ Tbsp vinegar and 1 ½ Tbsp soy sauce (taste)

Add chopped chives, bring stock to lively boil, then simmer.

Use 2 raw eggs for 4 people. Stream into stock as it is stirred.

For color and flavor add fresh spinach.

If no chives are available, use chopped leek in rounds or shavings.

Boil longer to cook – 2 minutes.

Serves 4

NOTES

Contributed by Ruth Holmes

Egg Drop Soup

PREPARATION TIME
NUMBER OF SERVINGS
SOURCE OF RECIPE — Gretchen

Chicken Bouillon 3 cups (2 cubes)
Add 1½ TB vinegar } taste
   " 1½ TB soy sauce }
Add chopped chives, bring stock to boil & simmer lively
Use 2 eggs (4 people), stream into stock as
it is stirred. For color + flavor add fresh spinach
If no chives, chopped leek in rounds or shavings
(boil longer to cook - 2 min)

Serve

STYLECRAFT, BALTO. 30. MD.   PRINTED IN U.S.A.
REFILL NO. 951

Clam Soup with Radish

INGREDIENTS

Sand clams ½ catty*
Radish cut into chunks 1/3 catty*

DIRECTIONS

Fry dried ginger in hot oil until fragrant; add clam meat and keep stir-frying; pour water and bring to the bowl. Add shredded radish; season with salt.

NOTES

* catty is a measurement that equals approximately 1.33 lbs or 604 g

Contributed by Mon Ho (Hong Kong)

Clam Soup with Radish

Ingredients

and clams   1/2 cattly
radish (cut into chunks)   1/3 cattly

teps :

) Fry dried ginger in hot oil until fragrent ; add clam mea
and keep stir-frying; pour water and bring to the boil.

Senate Bean Soup

DIRECTIONS

Soak 1 ½ lb pea or navy beans overnight in large bowl. Drain and let run under hot water until slightly whitened. Put beans in large soup pot and cover with 3 qt cold water.

Add 4 large onions and 1 large clove garlic, slightly browned in a little butter.

In a piece of cheesecloth tie a little bundle of the following:

6 stems parsley, ¾ tsp thyme, 1 ½ large bay leaves, 1 chopped carrot, ½ lemon. Add this bundle of herbs to beans.

Add 1 lbs smoked ham hocks or shank end of ham. Cover, cook slowly for 3 hours or til reduced by ½ and beans are done. Remove cheesecloth bag and discard. Remove ham and cool. Remove 2 cups beans with liquid and puree in blend or through a sieve. Return to pot with 2 cups of water. Remove ham, cut in small pieces and return to soup. Season to taste with salt and pepper. Reheat carefully.

Serve with hot corn bread and honey butter.

NOTES

Contributed by Juliana Martin via Sheila Lowe

What's cookin' Senate Bean Soup Serves 8
Recipe from the kitchen of Evelyn Martin

Put 1½ lb. pea or navy beans in large bowl, soak overnite. Drain beans and let run under hot water till slightly whitened. Put beans in large soup pot & cover with 3 qts. cold water. Add 4 large chopped onions & 1 large clove garlic that has been slightly browned in little butter. In piece of cheese cloth tie up in little bundle the following: 6 stems parsley, 3/4 tsp. thyme, 1½ lg. bay leaves, 1 chopped carrot, ½ lemon. Add this bundle of herbs to beans. Add 1 lb. ~~smoked~~ smoked Ham Hocks or shank end of ham. Cover cook slowly 3 hrs. or till reduced by ½ & beans are done. Remove cheesecloth bag & discard.

Senate Bean Soup (cont.)

Remove ham & cool. Remove 2c. beans with liquid. Puree in blender or thru sieve & return with 2c. water. Cut ham in small pieces & return to soup. Season to taste with salt & pepper. Reheat carefully.

Serve with hot corn bread & honey butter.

281

Dressed-up Crab Rangoon Dip

INGREDIENTS

12 oz cream cheese, softened
2 cans (6 oz each) crab meat, well-drained and any shells picked out.
3 scallions, chopped
2 Tbsp chopped sweet roasted red pepper
¾ shredded Swiss cheese
1/3 grated Parmesan cheese
1 tsp prepared horseradish
1 Tbsp Worcestershire sauce
1 Tbsp milk
¼ tsp garlic powder
¼ tsp salt
1/8 freshly ground pepper
2 Tbsp chopped slivered almonds
1 scallion, green part only, chopped for garnish

DIRECTIONS

Preheat oven to 375 degrees. Grease 8x8 baking dish. Mix together all ingredients except almonds and scallions. Transfer to prepared baking dish. Bake 20-25 minutes or until bubbly around edges. Top with almonds, bake 5 minutes more. Garnish with chopped green scallions.

NOTES

Third prize winner in 2015 Old Farmers Almanac Reader Recipe contest for dips and spreads: Debbie Reese, Clearwater, Florida

Contributed by Toria via Linda Larson

The Old Farmer's Almanac / Almanac.com   Beryl Toren 2022

makes 20 servings

Dressed-Up Crab Rangoon Dips

If you like Crab Rangoon, you will like this dip. In fact, I now prefer this dip to the appetizer itself.

12 oz   cream cheese, softened
2   cans (6 oz each) crabmeat, well drained and picked over for shells
3   scallions, chopped
2 Tbl   chopped sweet roasted red pepper
¾ C   shredded Swiss cheese
⅓ C   grated Parmesan cheese
1 tsp   prepared horseradish
1 Tbl   Worcestershire sauce
1 Tbl   milk
¼ tsp   garlic powder
¼ tsp   salt
⅛ tsp   freshly ground pepper
2 Tbl   chopped slivered almonds
1   scallion, green part only, chopped, for garnish

Preheat oven to 350° F .... and add garlic powder, salt & pepper.

In a bowl ... scallion ... horseradish ... Transfer mixture to prepared baking dish. Bake for 20 to 25 minutes, or until bubbly around edges. Top with almonds and bake for 5 minutes more.

Garnish with chopped green scallions.

Third-prize winner in 2015 Old Farmer's Almanac Reader Recipe Contest for dips & spreads. Debbie Reed, Clearwater, Florida

Submitted by Linda Larsen
Recipe from my friend, Toren (P178/R)

Mom's Tomato Sauce

INGREDIENTS

3 cans tomatoes (28 oz each)
2 gloves garlic
1 medium chopped onion
½ green pepper
olive oil
oregano

DIRECTIONS

Puree tomatoes in blender, put in pot and heat while sauteing garlic, peppers, and onion in olive oil.
Combine all of the above ingredients and simmer for as long as you like.
Add oregano. When you think you have enough oregano, add some more.
Add salt if you wish.

NOTES

Contributed by Kathleen Dickinson

Recipe: Tomato Sauce

From: mom   Makes: _____

3 cans tomatoes 28₃ each
2 gloves garlic
1 medium chopped onion
1/2 green pepper
olive oil
oregano
put cans of tomatoes in blender
& puree - put in pot & heat
        while
sauteeing garlic peppers & onions
in olive oil
combine all of the above & simmer
for as long as you like
add oregano   when you think
you have enough oregano   add
some more
add salt if you wish

285

Red Lobster Tartar Sauce

INGREDIENTS

1/3 cup miracle whip salad dressing
2/3 cup sour cream
¼ cup confectioners sugar
2 Tbsp sweet white onion chopped fine
2 Tbsp sweet pickle relish with juice
5 Tbsp carrot chopped fine
¼ tsp salt

DIRECTIONS

Chop the sweet onion in food processor and set aside.
Chop carrot in food processor and set aside.
Mix all ingredients in order listed and stir to blend well.
Refrigerate.

NOTES

I always use a lot more chopped carrot than called for.

Contributed by Tamara Tazzia (written at 23 years old)

RED LOBSTER TARTER SAUCE

- 1/3 CUP MIRACLE WHIP SALAD DRESSING
- 2/3 CUP SOUR CREAM
- 1/4 CUP CONFECTIONERS SUGAR
- 2 TBSP SWEET WHITE ONION (CHOPPED FINE)
- 2 TBSP SWEET PICKLE RELISH WITH JUICE
- 5 TBSP CARROT (CHOPPED FINE)
- 1/4 tsp SALT

- CHOP THE SWEET ONION IN FOOD PROCESSOR AND SET ASIDE.
- CHOP CARROT IN FOOD PROCESSOR AND SET ASIDE.
- MIX ALL INGREDIENTS IN ORDER LISTED AND STIR TO BLEND WELL.
- REFRIGERATE.

NOTE: I ALWAYS USE A LOT MORE CHOPPED CARROT THEN THEY CALL FOR.

Layered Oriental Dip

INGREDIENTS

1 cup chopped cooked chicken
½ shredded carrot
¼ cup chopped peanuts
3 Tbsp soy sauce, divided
1 tsp toasted sesame seeds
1 8 oz package cream cheese

DIRECTIONS

Combine top six ingredients only, using 2 Tbsp soy sauce.
Refrigerate.

Sauce:

2 Tbsp brown sugar
1 ½ tsp cornstarch
½ cup water, 2 Tbsp ketchup
1 ½ tsp Worcestershire sauce
1 tsp vinegar

In saucepan combine brown sugar and cornstarch, stir in
water, ketchup, Worcestershire sauce and vinegar. Bring to
a boil and cook 1 minute. Cool 5-10 minutes.

Smoosh cream cheese and 1 Tbsp soy sauce onto deep
dish pie plate. Cover with chicken mixture. Drizzle with
sauce. Serve with tortilla chips.

NOTES

Enjoy!

Contributed by Edda Manley

Layered Oriental Dip

1 c. chopped cooked chicken
1/2 c. shredded carrot
1/4 c. chopped peanuts
3 tbsp. soy sauce, divided
1 clove chopped garlic
1 tsp. toasted sesame seeds
1 8 oz. package cream cheese

Combine top six ingredients, only
using 2 tbsp. soy sauce. Refrigerate

Sauce: 2 tbsp. brown sugar
      1 1/2 tsp. corn starch
      1/2 c. water 2 tbsp. Ketchup
      1 1/2 tsp. Worcestershire sauce
      1 tsp. Vinegar
In saucepan combine brown sugar
and cornstarch, stir in water,
Ketchup, Worcestershire sauce and
Vinegar. Bring to a boil and cook
1 minute. Cool 5-10 minutes

Smoosh cream cheese and 1 tbsp.
soy sauce onto deep dish pie plate
Cover with chicken mixture. Drizzle
with sauce. Serve with tortilla chip

Enjoy!

Artichoke Dip / Spread

INGREDIENTS

1 cup mayonnaise (Hellmans)
1 cup grated Parmesan cheese
1 9 oz can artichoke hearts, roughly chopped
crushed garlic to taste
dash of Worcestershire sauce (optional)

DIRECTIONS

Combine ingredients and mix well. Spread into quiche or casserole dish. Bake 30 minutes at 350 degrees. Serve hot to warm.
Or bake 15 minutes at 375 degrees.
Serve with Brenner Crackers or toast rounds.

NOTES

Contributed by Ruth Holmes

Artichoke Dip (Spread) Preheat oven
                                    350°
1 cp. mayonaise (Hellmans)
1 cp. grated parmesan cheese
1 9g. can artichoke hearts - roughly
        chopped.
Crushed garlic to taste.
    dash of Worchester (optional)
Combine & mix well. Spread into quiche
or casserole dish. Bake for 30 min.
    Serve hot to warm.
Serve w. Bremner crackers or toast rounds.
    OR: Bake 15 min. @375°

Cream Sauce for Veggies

INGREDIENTS

½ cup butter
½ cup flour
½ cup dry milk
2 Tbsp onion powder
2 tsp salt
¼ tsp black pepper

DIRECTIONS

Cut butter into flour and add remaining ingredients. Mix until very crumbly. Refrigerate or freeze.
To use: Combine 2 cups vegetable and ½ cup water, bring to boil cover and cook until tender/crisp. Stir in 3 Tbsp mix, cooking til sauce thickens. Season with salt. Add herbs as desired – ¾ tsp of dried herbs for 2 cups of vegetables.

NOTES

Contributed by Sheila Lowe

Cream Sc mix for Veg.

½ C butter
½ C flour
½ C dry milk
2 T onion pdr.
2 t salt
¼ t. pepper.

cut butter into flour + rem. ingr. til
very crumbly. Refridgerate or freeze.

to use:

Combine 2 C Veg + ½ C wtr, bring to boil.
Cover & cook til tender/crisp. Stir in
3 T mix, cooking til Sc thickens. Season
w. salt.

add herbs as desired — ¾ t dried herbs/ for 2 C veg.

Salads & Vegetable Dishes

Mexican Watercress Orange Salad

INGREDIENTS

1 bunch watercress
Lettuce optional
1-2 oranges sliced or in chunks
1 sweet onion sliced or diced
2 avocado dipped in lemon juice
tomatoes may be substituted for oranges
2 Tbsp green chilis chopped
½ cup chopped pecans

Dressing
½ cup peanut oil
2 Tbsp olive oil
2 Tbsp lemon juice
juice of 1 orange
1 Tbsp honey

Prepare salad and refrigerate.

NOTES

Contributed by Tricia Clapp

Melisan Watercress Orange Salad

Watercress 1 bunch
lettuce - optional
1-2 Oranges sliced or in chunks
1 sweet onion sliced or diced
2 Avacado dipped in lemon juice
Tomatoe may be substituted for orange -
2 T Green Chilies chopped
1/2 C Chopped Pecans

Dressing
1/2 C Peanut Oil
2 T Olive Oil
2 T lemon juice
Juice of 1 orange
1 T Honey

Prepare salad and refrigerate

Fruit Ball

INGREDIENTS

1 pkg cream cheese (room temperature)
1 pkg coconut
1 cup pecans (chopped)
1 small can mandarin oranges (drained and chopped)
1 small can crushed pineapple (drained)
1 small box of vanilla pudding

DIRECTIONS

Mix cream cheese and fruit. Mix in vanilla pudding
powder. Mix in pecans. Chill. Form into a ball and roll in
coconut.
Serve with graham crackers, vanilla wafers, or ginger
snaps.

NOTES

This fruit ball is like a cheese ball for spreading.

(Ed. Note: in the absence of finding a photo of one big
fruit ball, the image is simply representative, not meant to
confuse the cook.)

Contributed by Kay Campbell via Helene Robinson

Fruit Ball

KAY CAMPBELL
HENDERSONVILLE NC

2 pkg cream cheese (room temp)
1 pkg coconut
1 cup pecans
1 sm. can mandarin oranges (drained & chopped)
1 sm can crushed pineapple (drained)
1 sm box vanilla pudding

- mix cream cheese & fruit - mix in vanilla pudding powder - mix in pecans - chill - then roll in coconut. Serve w/ graham crackers, vanilla wafers, or ginger snaps

Fried Okra

INGREDIENTS

3 cups sliced okra
1 cup cornmeal
½ cup flour
1 tsp salt
1 tsp pepper

DIRECTIONS

Combine cornmeal, flour, salt, pepper. Mix with sliced okra. Drop into hot oil in frying pan. Fry until brown.

NOTES

Contributed by Lib Porter via Helene Robinson

HERE'S WHAT'S COOKING: Fried Okra
FROM THE KITCHEN OF: LIB PORTER PICKENS, SC

3 C. sliced okra   1 C. cornmeal
1 t. salt   ½ C. flour
1 t. pepper

Add cornmeal, flour, salt, pepper
together. Mix with sliced okra.
Drop into hot oil in frying pan.
Fry until brown.

Akara – Nigerian Bean Cakes

INGREDIENTS

dried beans (In US black-eyed peas)
vegetable oil/palm oil
salt
seasoning cubes
onion (sliced/blended)
habanero pepper (dried or blended)
blended crayfish (optional)

DIRECTIONS

Soak beans to clean. Drain, puree with a little water, add onion and pepper. Slice the onion and pepper and add to beans. Pour into a bowl, add salt and seasoning power. Add sliced onion and pepper (if desired). Add blended crayfish. Stir all together to mix well and taste good. Heat frying pan, add vegetable or palm oil, heat for a few minutes, then add the puree and fry on medium heat. When browned remove from oil. Serve hot with any of the items listed in the notes below.

NOTES

Akara (Local name in Yoruba language) is a staple, and common food in Nigeria liked by both children and adults, and cuts across the different tribes. It can be eaten alone or combined with pap (from dry corn), custard, oats, Gaari (made from cassava), tea beverage. Bread, fried yam, fried plantain.

Contributed by Mrs. Oladipupo Macjob

Akara — Bean Cakes/Bean Balls

Akara (local name in yoruba language)
It is a stable and common food in Nigeria liked by both
children and adults and it cuts across all the different
tribes in Nigeria.
It can be eaten alone or combined with pap (made from
dry corn), Custard, O___ ___ari (made from cassava), Tea,
beverage, bread, f___ ___ plantain

Preparation

Ingredients:

- Beans
- Vegetable
- Salt
- Seasoning Cubes
- Onion (sliced/blended)
- pepper - Habanero pepper (sliced or
- blended Crayfish (optional)

Then add in a bowl, add Salt and Seasoning powder.
Also add the sliced onion and pepper (if desired)
Add the blended crayfish.
Sti__ all together till they all mix well and taste well
Then, put your frying pan on fire, add groundnut vegetable
oil or palm oil, allow it to heat for few minutes, then add
the puree in sizeable content, fry on medium heat
Then when brown as desired and bring out of oil
Serve while it is hot with any of the listed above.

Preparation

Take the desired measured of beans, pick the dirts
and peel off the coverings of the beans in water.
Blend with little water, add onion and pepper to the
beans and blend together.
You can also slice the onion and pepper and add to the
blended beans if you desire not to blend

Sesame Noodle Salad

INGREDIENTS

2 lbs cooked vermicelli pasta
¾ cup sesame oil
Minced garlic to taste
½ Tbsp minced ginger
1 cup sugar
2 bunches chopped green onion
¼ cup hoisin sauce
2+ Tbsp rice wine vinegar
1/8 cup honey
½ cup toasted sesame seeds

DIRECTIONS

Combine and refrigerate for an hour or until cold. It serves a lot of people.

NOTES

Long ago, I moved from California to New Jersey and worked at a deli. Three days into my employment, one young coworker (a 17 year-old girl) asked, "Hey! Are you a vegetarian or something, because you don't know sh** about meat?!" I laughed, and she was right. I didn't know much about meat, but I am not a vegetarian. But there was a wonderful sesame noodle salad that one of the chefs made and I thought was fabulous.

Contributed by Linda Larson

Long ago (moved from California to New Jersey and worked at a
Deli. 2 days into my employment, one of my Co-workers (a 19yr
old girl) asked "Hey! are you a vegetarian or something, be
cause you don't know SH*XX!! about meat !?!" I laughed
But There was a wonderful SESSAME NOODLE SALAD. and she was right
That one of The Chefs made I Thought was fabulous.

<u>Sessame Noodle Salad</u> / for a lot of people

2 LBS vermicelli pasta (cooked)
3/4 cup Sesame oil   I didn't know
Minced garlic to taste   much about meat,
1/2 TBLsp minced ginger   but I am not a
1 cup Sugar   vegetarian
2 Bunches green onions, chopped
1/4 cup hosin Sauce
2 + TBLS Rice Wine vinegar
1/8 cup honey
1/2 cup Sesame seeds (toasted)

Combine + leave in Refrig for an hour or until
Cold.

Corn Pudding

INGREDIENTS

1 15 ¼ oz can of whole kernel corn, drained
1 14 ¾ oz cream style corn
1 8 oz pkg Jiffy cornbread mix (yep the cheap stuff!)
1 cup sour cream + 2 Tbsp milk
½ cup melted butter
1 - 1 ½ cup shredded cheddar cheese
3 eggs
1-2 tsp cornstarch
1 jar pimientos for color and sparkle

DIRECTIONS

Grease/spray a 1 quart casserole dish.
Combine all ingredients, pour into dish and bake for 45-50 minutes at 325 - 350 degrees until firm (it should not jiggle)
Let stand 5 minutes before serving.

NOTES

This is my best and most well-received recipe ever! It is always requested and so easy to make, it's almost embarrassing. One of the great 'comfort' recipes.

Contributed by Linda Larson

Oven 325°-350°   CORN PUDDING
Bake 48-50 min

This is one of the best and most well received recipes ever!
Temp 325°-350°
Grease/spray a 2 quart Casserol Dish

1 (15¼ oz) Can of whole Kernel Corn (Drained)
1 (14¾ oz) Cream-styled Corn
1 (8 oz) pkg Jiffy Corn mix (yep - The cheap stuff!)
1 cup Sour Cream + 2 TBLS Milk
½ cup Melted Butter
1 - 1½ cup shredded Cheddar Cheese
3 Eggs
1-2 tsp Cornstarch
1 jar of pimentos (for color and sparkle

Bake for 45-50 minutes at 325°-350° (until firm
Let stand 5 minutes b/4 serving   (it should not
                                                            jiggle

This is The most favourite all time Thing I have ever cooked,
"hands (or pans) down"! It is always is requested and
is so easy to make, it's almost embarassing! One of
The great "Comfort" recipes.
                                                    Linda L.

307

Funeral Potatoes

INGREDIENTS

16 oz shredded potatoes (frozen, but thawed)
½ cup sour cream
1 tsp garlic
¾ cup diced (cooked) onion
1 ¼ cup cheddar cheese, shredded
2 eggs, blended
6 Tbsp butter
Salt/pepper

DIRECTIONS

In a large bowl, mix soup, sour cream, cheese, eggs, butter and salt and pepper.
Stir in thawed potatoes, just until mixed.
Spray baking pan and pour in mix.
Spread 1 cup crushed cornflakes on top, mixed with 1-2 Tbsp melted butter.
Cover top with foil and bake 35 minutes. Take off foil the last 10 minutes until brown.
(Could add chicken if desired).

NOTES

I lived in upper, upper, upper NY for a while and was told that this is **the** casserole recipe to bring to any gathering. It really is the dish that shows up when people are brought food during difficult times. It obviously generated from the 1950s

Contributed by Linda Larson

FUNERAL POTATOES (½ recipe)

I lived in upper, upper, upper NY for awhile and was told that *this* is THEE casserole recipe to bring to any gathering, and it really with dish that shows up when people are brought food during difficult times. It obviously generated from the 1950's.

Oven 350°

6 g Potatoes (frozen shredded, but Thawed)
10 g Cream of Chicken Soup
½ cup Sour cream
1 tsp garlic
¾ cup diced onion (cooked)
1¼ cup Cheddar Cheese, shredded
2 eggs, blended
6 TBLS butter
Salt / Pepper

- Large bowl, mix soup, sour cream, cheese, eggs, butter & salt & pepper
- Stir in Thawed potatoes, just till mixed
- Spray baking pan & pour in mix.
- Spread (1 cup corn flakes (crushed) on TOP)
  (mixed with 1-2 TBLS melted butter)
- Cover top w/foil & bake 35 minutes
- take off foil The last 10 minutes, until brown

[could add chicken.]

Stuffed Tomatoes

INGREDIENTS

6 Tomatoes
½ cup butter
1/3 cup onion
1 tsp basil leaves
1 tsp salt
2 Tbsp parsley
¼ tsp pepper
1 cup bread crumbs

DIRECTIONS

(Ed. Note: No directions were given, so what I would do is: scoop out the tomato pulp and combine the ingredients above. Stuff the tomatoes and bake 20 to 30 minutes at 350 degrees. I would also add grated cheddar cheese.)

NOTES

Contributed by Carla Winter

STUFFED TOMATOES

6 TOM   1 tsp Basil leaves
  ½ C. BUTTER
  1 CHOPPED ONION
  3C   1 tsp Salt

2 TABLS Parsley ¼ tsp pepper
1 cup Bread crumbs.

Cowboy Candy (candied peppers)

INGREDIENTS

1 ½ lbs jalapenos (about 30)
1 cup apple cider vinegar
3 cups sugar
1 tsp garlic powder
¼ tsp turmeric
¼ tsp celery seed

DIRECTIONS

Remove/discard stems from peppers, then slice to ¼"
slices, set aside. To a large pot, add vinegar, sugar, garlic
powder, turmeric, and celery seed, bring to a boil. Reduce
heat to medium-low and simmer for 5 minutes.

Raise heat to medium-high to bring mixture back to a
boil. Once boiling, add peppers. Return to a boil, then
reduce heat to medium-low and simmer for 4 minutes.

Transfer peppers with slotted spoon to clean glass jars,
filling to within ¼" of rim.

Only syrup should be in pot. Increase heat to full rolling
boil for approximately 6 minutes.

Ladle syrup into jars. Use spoon to get rid of any air
pockets. Fill jars to within ¼ - ½" from rim.

Wipe rims with damp paper towel, screw on lids.

Refrigerate at least 1-2 weeks (3-4 weeks optional). Good
for 3 months refrigerated.

Ed. Note: wear gloves when handling jalapenos!

Contributed by Tara Porter via Helene Robinson

HERE'S WHAT'S COOKING: Cowboy Candy
FROM THE KITCHEN OF: Candied Peppers

1 1/2 lbs. jalapeños (about 30)
1 cup apple cider vinegar
3 cups sugar
1 tsp garlic powder
1/4 tsp tumeric
1/4 tsp celery seeds

1) Remove/discard stems from peppers, then slice into 1/4" slices, set aside.
2) To a large pot, add cider vinegar, white sugar, garlic powder, turmeric, and celery

HERE'S WHAT'S COOKING: seed and bring to a
FROM THE KITCHEN OF: boil. Reduce heat to about MED LOW and simmer for 5 minutes.
3) Raise heat to MED HIGH to bring mixture back to a boil. Once boiling, add peppers. Allow to return to boil then reduce heat to MED LOW and simmer for 4 minutes.
4) Transfer peppers w/slotted spoon to clean glass jars, filling to within 1/4 inch of rim.
5) Only syrup should be in pot. Increase heat to full rolling boil. Boil for approx.
6) min

6.) Ladle syrup into jars. Use spoon to get rid of any air pockets. Fill jars to within 1/4 - 1/2" from upper rim.

7) Wipe rims of jars with damp paper towel, screw on lids. Refridgerate for at least 1-2 weeks (3-4 weeks optimal). Good for 3 months refrigerated.

Cranberry Salad

INGREDIENTS

1 cup raw ground cranberries
1 pkg frozen strawberries
1 pkg strawberry jello
1 Tbsp Knox gelatin dissolved in ¼ cup cold water
1 cup crushed pineapple
2 cups boiling water
1 cup sugar
1 cup chopped nuts

DIRECTIONS

Dissolve strawberry jello in hot water. Add dissolved gelatin. Stir in sugar until dissolved. Add pineapple with juices. Chill until it begins to thicken. Add berries. Nuts may be added to jello or put on top.
Beat ½ cup sour half and half (cream) and 2 Tbsp mayo and 2 Tbsp Dream Whip. Fill center of ring mold.

NOTES

Contributed by Mary Shanks via Tricia Clapp

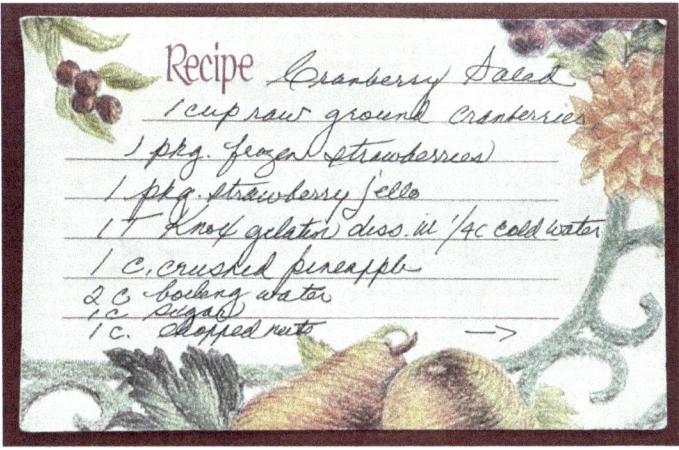

Recipe Cranberry Salad

1 cup raw ground cranberries
1 pkg. frozen strawberries
1 pkg. strawberry jello
1 T Knox gelatin diss. in 1/4 c cold water
1 c. crushed pineapple
2 c. boiling water
1 c. sugar
1 c. chopped nuts ⟶

Dissolve Strawberry jello in hot water.
Add dissolved gelatin. Stir sugar until
dissolved. Add pineapple with juices. Chill
until it begins to thicken. Add berries
Nuts may be added to jello or put on top.
In center of ring mold —
Beat 1/2 cup sour beef & beef and 2 T mayo
and 2 T dream whip. (dream)

Enjoy —
Mary Shanks.

Sharon's Zucchini Tots

INGREDIENTS

2 cups packed grated zucchini - put in bowl with 1 Tbsp salt and set aside.
2 cups grated carrots
½ cup finely chopped onion
1 Tbsp parsley
2 eggs beaten
1 cup flour
1 tsp baking powder
½ tsp celery salt; garlic
1 cup grated Parmesan cheese

DIRECTIONS

Drain liquid from zucchini after 10 minutes. Mix together remaining ingredients. Shape into 2 Tbsp sized tots and brown both sides in skillet.
Can be served with sour cream or salsa, warm or at room temperature.

NOTES

Tip: When each batch is browned, place on cookie sheet in 350 deg. Oven. Cool and refrigerate. Can be heated before serving.
Each batch makes 30 average-sized tots.

Contributed by Edda Manley

Sharon's Zucchini Tots

2 c. packed grated zucchini
   (put in bowl with 1 tbsp salt
    and set aside)
2 c. grated carrots
½ c. onions
1 tblsp. parsley
2 eggs beaten
1 c. flour
1 tsp. baking powder
½ tsp. celery salt; garlic
1 c. grated parmeasan

Drain liquid from zucchini after
10 min.
Mix together remaining ingredients
Shape into 2 tblsp. sized tots
and brown both sides in skillet
Can be served with sour cream or
salsa sauce, warm or at room
temperature.

TIP: When each batch is browned
     place on cookie sheet in 350°
     oven. Cool and refrigerate.
     Can be heated before serving

Each Batch makes 29 large 30 avg
                              tots

Jen's Sweet Potato Casserole

INGREDIENTS

3 cups mashed sweet potatoes

1 cup sugar

½ tsp vanilla

1 cup coconut

1 stick butter

Mix these ingredients together and pour into a casserole dish.

DIRECTIONS

Mix and pour over sweet potato mixture:

1 stick butter

1 cup brown sugar

1 cup pecans

½ cup flours

Mix these ingredients together and pour over potato mixture.

Bake for 20 + minutes at 350 degrees.

NOTES

Finding this recipe in the handwriting of my daughter was a bittersweet gift. She loved cooking and had a collection of cookbooks that I distributed to family members when she was killed. One of my favorite photos was taken on a Thanksgiving holiday where she and my older son were cooking a turkey together.

Contributed by Sheila Lowe on behalf of her late daughter Jennifer Lowe

Sweet Potato Casserole

3 c mashed Sweet Potatoes
1 c Sugar
½ c evaporated milk
2 t Vanilla
1 c. Coconut
1 Stick butter

Bake @ 350 for 20+ minutes

mix & Pour over Potato mixture
1 Stick butter
1 c. Brown Sugar
1 c Pecans, ½ c flour

Purple Cabbage Comfort

DIRECTIONS

Brown 1 lb ground beef with onions and garlic. Drain fat and add 1 large can diced tomatoes. Layer, starting with purple cabbage.

Make at 350 degrees until bubbly.

This dish freezes well. If frozen, cook for about an hour.

NOTES

A sweet painting by Peg's granddaughter.

Contributed by Peg Brantley

Purple Cabbage Comfort
Brown hamburger
w/onions & garlic. Drain
and add 1 large can
diced tomatoes. Layer,
starting with purple
cabbage. 350° til
bubbly. Freezes well—
if frozen, about 1 hr.

Swiss Vegetable Medley

INGREDIENTS

1 bag (16 oz) combined frozen broccoli, carrots, cauliflower, thawed and drained (I also added a 9 oz pkg).
1 can condense cream of mushroom soup.
1 cup shredded Swiss cheese (or the kind you like)
1/3 cup sour cream
¼ tsp ground pepper
1 jar (4 oz) chopped pimiento, drained (optional)
1 can (2.8 oz) Durkee's French Fried Onions

DIRECTIONS

Combine vegetables, soup, ½ cup cheese, sour cream, pepper, pimiento and ½ can French Fried Onions. Pour into a 1 qt casserole dish. Bake, covered, for 30 minutes at 350 deg. Top with remaining cheese and onions; bake, uncovered for 5 minutes longer. Makes six servings.

Alternative *Microwave* directions:

Prepare as above. Cook, covered, for 12 minutes on high. Stir and turn halfway through. Top with remaining cheese and onions. Cook uncovered 1 minutes or until the cheese melts.

NOTES

Contributed by Kim Woodward

RECIPE FOR **Swiss Vegetable Medley**

1 bag (16 oz.) Frozen Broccoli, Carrots, + Cauliflower Combination, thawed + drained (I also added a 9 oz. pkg.)
1 can Condensed Cream of Mushroom Soup
1 cup shredded Swiss Cheese (or kind you like)
1/3 C. Sour Cream
1/4 t. Ground Pepper
1 jar (4 oz.) Chopped pimento, drained (optional)
1 can (2.8 oz.) Durkee's French Fried Onions

Combine veg., soup, 1/2 c. cheese, Sour Cream, pepper, pimiento and 1/2 can French Fried Onions. Pour into a 1 qt. Casserole. Bake, covered at 350° for 30 mins. Top with remaining cheese + onions; bake, uncovered 5 mins. longer. (6 Servings)

Microwave Directions: Prepare as above. Cook, covered on High 12 mins. Stir + turn, halfway through. Top w/ remaining cheese + onions. Cook uncovered 1 minute or until cheese melts.

Jackie Olden's Potato Casserole

INGREDIENTS

6 potatoes, boiled
2 cup shredded cheese
¼ cup melted butter
onion, grated
1 tsp salt
2 cups sour cream, room temperature
2 Tbsp butter

DIRECTIONS

Peel cooled potatoes and shred. Gently toss with cheese and remaining ingredients. Bake 25 minutes at 325 degrees.

NOTES

Written when I was very young and lacking in self-confidence(!)

Contributed by Sheila Lowe

Potato Casserole

Jackie
Oldem

6 potatoes, baked
2 C shredded cheese
¼ C melted butter.
    Onion
1 t salt
2 C sour cream - room temp.
2 T butter.

Peel cooked pot. shred. Toss w. cheese
add sour. Bkg. quickly 325° 25 min

Gullivers Corn au Gratin

INGREDIENTS

1 lb frozen or canned corn
1 ½ cup whipping cream
1 ½ Tbsp clarified butter
1 ½ Tbsp flour
½ tsp salt
2 Tbsp sugar
½ tsp Accent seasoning
3 Tbsp Parmesan cheese

DIRECTIONS

Add corn to cream, bring to a boil. Strain and put the cream back on. Make a roux with the flour and butter. Simmer on stove for 5 minutes. Season with salt. Add other ingredients to sauce. Bring to boil, add the corn. Put in casserole, sprinkle with cheese. Brown under broiler.
4 servings

NOTES

This recipe came from Gulliver's restaurant in Orange County, CA in the 1970s. I just learned they are still in Irvine. Maybe worth a trip.

Contributed by Sheila Lowe

Gulliver's

Corn Au Gratin

1 LB corn
1½ C whipping cream
1½ T clarified butter
1½ T flour
½ t salt
2 T sug.
½ t accent.
3 T parmesan cheese

Put corn in cream. bring to boil. Strain. put cream back on. make roux (flour + butter) Simmer 5 mins ♪

Season   salt   add to Sauce bring
                  Sug
to boil   accent.   Add corn   put in
casserole.   ~~let cheese add corn~~ Put
Sprinkle w. cheese. brown under broiler

4 servings

Sweet Kosher Dills

DIRECTIONS

1 qt kosher dills, sliced. Drain but leave pickles in jar.

Boil for 1 minute:
2 cups sugar
½ cup water
½ cup cider vinegar
½ dozen whole cloves

Pour over sliced dills, which have been returned to jar. Refrigerate for 2-3 days.

NOTES

Contributed by Ruth Holmes

Another surprise from the kitchen of: M KURTA

Recipe for: Sweet/Kosher Dills

1 QT. KOSHER DILLS- SLICED
DRAIN BUT LEAVE PICKLES IN JAR
2 c sugar
1/2 c WATER
1/2 c CIDER VINEGAR   } Boil
1/2 DOZEN WHOLE CLOVES   } 1 minute
POUR OVER SLICED DILLS WHICH
HAVE BEEN RETURNED TO JAR
REFRIG. FOR 2-3 DAYS

Sunshine Salad

INGREDIENTS

1 pkg lemon flavored gelatin (jello)
1 cup hot water
1 cup pineapple syrup and water
1 Tbsp vinegar
½ tsp salt
1 cup grated raw carrots
2 ½ cups crushed canned pineapple, drained
½ cup chopped pecans

DIRECTIONS

Dissolve gelatin in hot water. Add pineapple syrup, water, vinegar and salt. Chill until slightly thickened. Fold carrots, pineapple, nuts into slightly thickened gelatin.
Turn into individual molds or 10 x 6 x 1 ½ pan.
Chill until firm.
Unmold on crisp lettuce. Garnish with mayonnaise.
6 servings

NOTES

Contributed by Ruth Holmes

Sunshine Salad

1 pkg lemon flavored gelatin (Jello)
1 cup hot water
1 cup pineapple syrup and water
1 tablespoon vinegar
1/2 teaspoon salt
1 cup grated raw carrots
1 No. 2 can (2 1/2 cups) crushed pineapple, drained
1/2 cup chopped pecans

Dissolve gelatine in hot water. Add pineapple syrup, water, vinegar & salt. Chill till slightly thickened. Fold carrots, pineapple & nuts into slightly thickened gelatine. Turn into individual molds or 10 x 6 x 1 1/2" pan. Chill till firm. Unmold on crisp lettuce. Garnish with mayonnaise. 6 servings.

Succotash

INGREDIENTS

1 pkg (10 oz) frozen lima beans
2 Tbsp butter
½ cup chopped onion
½ cup diced red bell pepper
1 pkg (10 oz) frozen corn thawed, or 1 can Niblets and 1 can creamed corn
1 tsp paprika
½ tsp garlic salt
½ tsp whole thyme
¼ tsp coarse ground pepper
½ cup heavy cream (optional)

DIRECTIONS

Cook lima beans per pkg directions until tender. Drain and set aside.

Melt butter in large nonstick skillet on medium heat. Add onion and bell pepper; cook and stir 7 minutes or until tender.

Stir in Lima beans, corn, paprika, garlic salt, thyme and pepper until well mixed. Reduce heat to low; cover and simmer 3 - 5 minutes or until vegetables are heated through.

*For creamier dish, add ½ cup heavy cream with the corn.

Contributed by Tara Porter via Helene Robinson

HERE'S WHAT'S COOKING: Succotash
FROM THE KITCHEN OF: Sara Porter Pickens, SC

1 package (10 oz) frozen lima beans
2 tablespoons butter
1/2 cup chopped onion
1/2 cup diced red bell pepper
1 package (10 oz) frozen corn thawed
   or 1 can niblets and 1 can creamed corn
1 teaspoon Paprika
1/2 teaspoon garlic salt
1/2 teaspoon whole thyme
1/4 teaspoon Coarse ground black pepper
* 1/2 cup heavy cream (optional)

HERE'S WHAT'S COOKING:
FROM THE KITCHEN OF:

1. Cook lima beans per pkg directions until tender. Drain and set aside.
2. Melt butter in large nonstick skillet on medium heat. Add onion and bell pepper; Cook and stir 7 minutes or until tender.
3. Stir in lima beans, corn, paprika, garlic salt, thyme and pepper until well mixed. Reduce heat to low; cover and simmer 3 to 5 minutes or until vegetables are heated through.
4)* For creamier dish, add 1/2 heavy cream with the corn)

333

Chicons – Belgian Endive

INGREDIENTS

3 chicons (Belgian endive), cleaned and separated
cleaned spinach leaves.
pecans
julienne beets
watercress if available
grated hard boiled egg
Any other "cool" additions (chopped cucumber, seeded
tomato, etc.)

DIRECTIONS

Toss all at last minute with vinaigrette dressing:
Lemon juice, olive oil (1:3). Add a little Dijon mustard
and chopped parsley.
Let sit. Remember salt and freshly ground pepper.

NOTES

From Josette's cooking class, Brussels.

Contributed by Ruth Holmes

Recipe

Serves 6

3 endives – cleaned & separated
cleaned spinach leaves – pecans – julienne
beets – watercress if available – grated
hard boiled egg – any other "cool" additions
(chopped cucumber, seeded tomato, etc)

Toss all at last minute with
vinaigrette dressing: lemon juice & olive
oil (1:3) And a little dijon mustard and
chopped parsley. Shake & let sit beneath
salt and freshly ground pepper

Source Josette's cooking class – Brussels

335

Joyce's Baked Mushrooms

INGREDIENTS

2 lbs large fresh mushroom caps
1 ½ cups melted butter
2 tsp chopped onions
1 clove garlic, minced or pressed
¾ tsp Worcestershire sauce
½ tsp dried rosemary
½ tsp each salt and pepper

DIRECTIONS

Mix butter with all seasoning.
Arrange mushroom caps, cut side up in large shallow baking dish. Pour seasoned butter over mushrooms.
Bake uncovered for 40 minutes at 325 degrees.

NOTES

Contributed by Ruth Holmes

Here's what's cookin: **Baked Mushrooms**

Recipe from the kitchen of

Joyce

2 lbs large fresh mushroom caps

1½ c. melted butter

2 tsp. chopped onions

1 clove garlic, minced or pressed

¾ tsp. worchestershire sauce

½ tsp. dried rosemary

½ tsp. each salt + pepper

Mix butter with all seasonings.

Serves ____

Arrange mushroom caps, cut side up, in large shallow baking dish.

Pour seasoned butter over mushrooms

Bake uncovered at 325° for 40 min.

Balsamic Dressing

INGREDIENTS

4 shallots
2 bunches basil, picked
½ Jamaican sugar, sugar in the raw
10 cloves garlic, roasted
3 cups balsamic reduced to 1 cup
2 tsp tomato paste
1 ½ cups water
3 cups salad oil
Pinch of salt and pepper to taste

DIRECTIONS

Reduce the 3 cups of balsamic to 1 cup. Place shallots and sugar in food processor. Roast garlic then add with salt, pepper, basil. Add tomato paste, water and vinegar. Slowly drizzle oil in while processor is on until emulsified. Adjust seasoning to taste.

Salad
Heat up dressing slowly, add bacon. Once hot, pour over salad and add blue cheese.

NOTES

Contributed by Peg Brantley

Balsamic Dressing
Yield: 2½ qts.

4 pc	shallots
2 bunches	basil, picked
½ cup	jamaican sugar, sugar in the raw
10 cloves	garlic, roasted
3 c	balsamic vin., reduced to 1 c
2 tsp	tomato paste
1½ c	water
3 c	salad oil
To taste	Salt & Pepper (pinch of each)

Reduce the 3 cups of balsamic to 1c.
In food processor put shallots and sugar.
Roast Garlic then Add w/ S & P and basil processor.
Add tomato paste, H₂O and vinegar.
Slowly drizzle oil in while processor is on until emulsified.
Adjust seasoning to taste.

Salad
Heat up dressing slowly, add bacon th
once hot pour over salad and add
bleu cheese.

341

Tanya's Homemade Hummus

INGREDIENTS

2 Tbsp olive oil
1 tin (15 oz) garbanzo beans, strained and rinsed–keep the liquid.1/3 cup tahini (a little less is better), ½ tsp salt
1 small garlic clove
3 Tbsp lemon juice (can add more to taste)

DIRECTIONS

Pour ingredients into a blender. Add 6 Tbsp liquid - half water, half garbanzo bean liquid.
Blend till smooth, add more liquid, a little at a time. Add more salt or lemon juice to taste - adjust the consistency as desired.
Serve with warm pita bread wedges and veggies.

NOTES

You'll never use store-bought hummus again!

Contributed by Tanya Jorgenson

Homemade Hummus
2 Tablespoons Olive oil
1 tin garbanzo beans (15 oz) strained and rinsed - keep the liquid.
1/3 cup tahini - (a little less is better), 1/2 tsp salt
1 small garlic clove.
3 tablespoons lemon juice (can add more to taste

Pour ingredients into a blender. Add 6 tablespoons liquid - half water, half garbanzo bean liquid.
Blend till smooth - add more liquid, a little at a time. Add more salt or lemon juice to taste - adjust the consistency as desired.
Serve with warm pita bread wedges and veggies.
You'll never use store-bought hummus again!
Tanya Torgeson

Poppyseed Dressing

INGREDIENTS

½ cup sugar
1 tsp dry mustard
1 tsp salt
1 ½ Tbsp onion juice
1 cup oil
1 cup vinegar
1 ½ Tbsp poppy seed

DIRECTIONS

Mix sugar, mustard, salt and vinegar together. Gradually add oil, beating constantly. Add poppy seed last.
Makes about 2 cups.
Do not use a blender!

NOTES

Contributed by Peg Brantley

Poppy Seed Dressing

1/2 c. sugar
1 tsp. dry mustard
1 tsp. salt
1 1/2 T. onion juice
1 c. oil
1 c. vinegar
1 1/2 T. poppy seed

Mix sugar, mustard, salt and vinegar together. Gradually add oil, beating constantly. Add poppy seed last.

Makes about 2 cups.

(Use _no_ blender)

Quick Pizza Sauce

INGREDIENTS

3 Tbsp EVOO
2 garlic cloves, minced
(¼ cup grated onion - use large holes on box grater–
optional)
1 28 oz can crushed tomatoes (Hunts or Cento–harder to
find)
salt and pepper
shredded fresh basil, if available

DIRECTIONS

Heat oil, onion if using, and garlic in medium saucepan
over medium heat. Cook until onions soften for 5-7
minutes. If not using onion, cook garlic in oil for 1 ½ - 2
minutes until sizzling.
Stir tomatoes and simmer until sauce thickens for 15
minutes. Remove from heat, stir in salt and pepper, then
basil, if using.
May be prepared and refrigerated up to four days in
advance.

NOTES

From *America's Test Kitchen Family Cookbook,* page 476

Contributed by Peg Brantley

Quick Pizza Sauce
 3 Cups, enough for 3 pizzas
 20 minutes start to finish

3 T. EVOO
2 garlic cloves, minced
{ ¼ C. grated onion - use large holes on Box grater - optional}
1 28g can crushed tomatoes (Hunts or Cento - harder to find)
   Salt + Pepper
{shredded fresh basil, if available}

Heat oil, onion if using, + garlic in med. saucepan over
med. heat. Cook until onions soften @ 5-7 min. if not using
onion cook garlic in oil @ 1½-2 minutes until sizzling.
Stir in tomatoes + simmer until sauce thickens, @ 15 min.
Off heat, stir in salt + pepper, then basil, if using.

May be prepared + refrigerated up to 4 days in advance!

America's Test Kitchen Family Cookbook
            p. 476

347

Debbie's Artichoke Dip

INGREDIENTS

1 can (15 oz) artichoke hearts, chopped
1 can (4 oz) chopped green chili
mayonnaise (best to use between ¼ - ½ cup)
¼ - ½ cup Parmesan cheese

DIRECTIONS

Mix and place in a casserole dish. Bake for 30 minutes at 350 degrees.
Serve with Tortilla chips
Serves 6

NOTES

This is a super dip—will get many compliments!

Contributed by Peg Brantley

Recipe from: Debbie
Date: January 1987

Artichoke Dip
(Excellent !!!!)

1 can (about 15oz) artichoke
 hearts - chopped.
1-4oz can chopped green-chilis
1/4 - 1/2 cup Mayonnaise
 (best to use in between)
 1/4 - 1/2 cup)
1/4 - 1/2 cup parmesan cheese

Mix and bake at 350°
for 30 minutes in
a casserole dish.

Serves 6.

Serve with Tortilla Chips

This is a superb dip —
will get many complements

Serves:

349

Grilled Chicken Marinade

INGREDIENTS

½ cup olive oil
1 tsp sea salt
½ tsp ground black pepper
½ tsp paprika
½ tsp cumin
¼ tsp cayenne pepper
2 cloves garlic, chopped
3 Tbsp chopped onion
½ cup chopped fresh parsley
½ cup beer

DIRECTIONS

Pour olive oil into a 2-cup liquid measuring cup.
Mix together salt, pepper, paprika, cumin and cayenne,
and add to olive oil. Mix well with fork. Slowly add beer.
Add chicken. Marinate 1 hour.

NOTES

Contributed by Peg Brantley

Grilled Chicken Marinade

1/2 c olive oil
1 t sea salt
1/2 t ground black pepper
1/2 t paprika
1/2 t cumin
1/4 t cayenne pepper
2 cloves garlic, chopped
3 T chopped onion
1/3 c chopped fresh parsley
1 1/2 c beer

1. Pour olive oil into a 2-cup liquid measuring cup
2. Mix together salt, pepper, paprika, cumin & cayenne and add to oil. Mix well w/fork. Slowly add beer
3. Add chicken — 1 hr.

Beverages

Mrs Scott's 5-Star Tequila

INGREDIENTS

1 cup Mr & Mrs T's mix
1/3 cup tequila
1/3 cup triple sec or orange curacao
2 tsp powdered sugar
15 ice cubes

DIRECTIONS

Place in blender and blend until frothy

NOTES

Contributed by Peg Brantley

Mrs' Scott's 5 ✳ Recipe

1 cup Mr + Mrs T's Mix

⅓ cup tequila

⅓ cup triple sec or
     orange curacao

2 tsp powdered sugar

15 ice cubes
≡
blender until frothy

Yooper Slush

INGREDIENTS

9 cups water
2 cups sugar
8 green tea bags
12 oz frozen orange juice
12 oz frozen lemonade
3 cups whiskey

DIRECTIONS

Steep tea bags in 2 cups water for 15 minutes. Discard bags.
Dissolve sugar in tea
In large container (bowl) combine tea mixture, remaining water, lemonade and whiskey. Stir until fully dissolved.
Place in freezer for 36 hours.
Serve in glasses - scrape frozen mixture.

NOTES

A boozy slush recipe from my grandmother who was born and raised in Michigan's Upper Peninsula. The peeps in the UP are referred to as *Yoopers*. Not a derogatory term, but rather a prideful label.

Contributed by Ron Lawrence

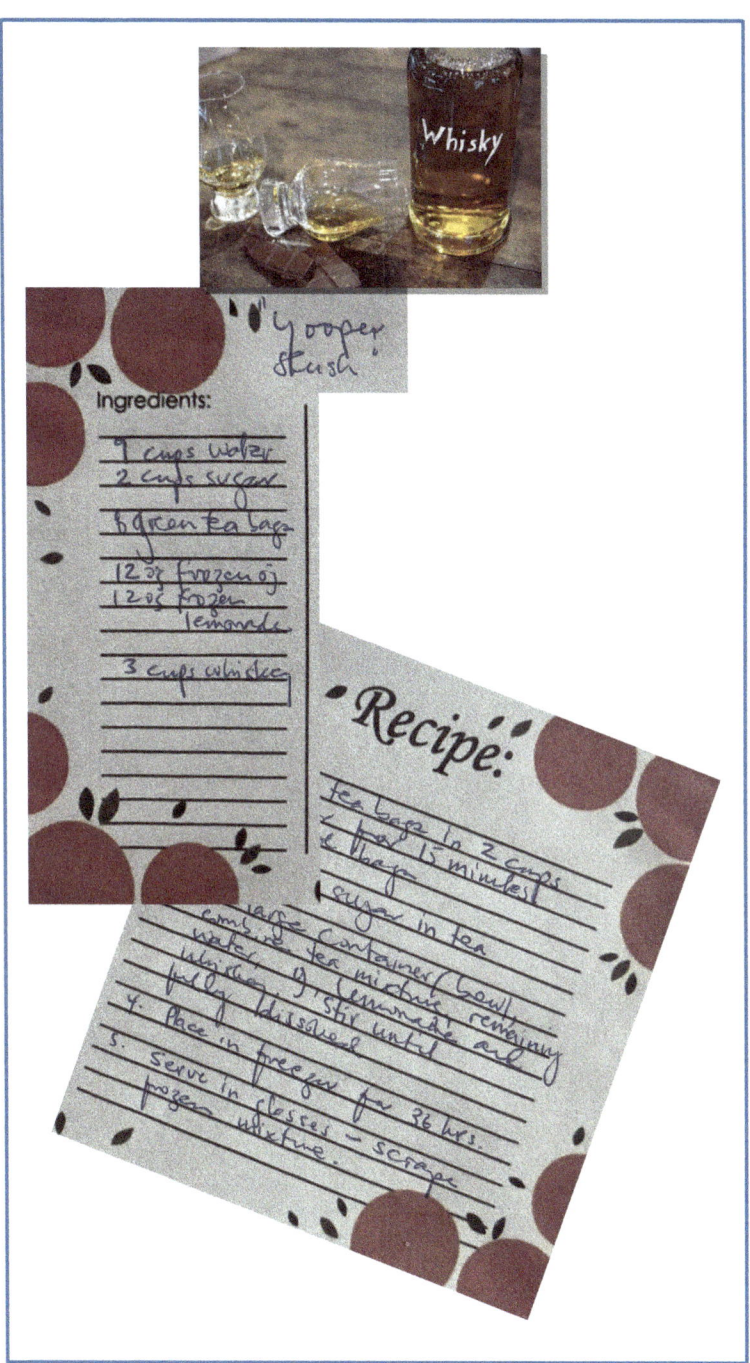

"Yooper slush"

Ingredients:

9 cups water
2 cups sugar
6 green tea bags
12 oz frozen oj
12 oz frozen lemonade
3 cups whiskey

Recipe:

1. Tea bags in 2 cups water 15 minutes & 4 bags
2. sugar in tea
3. large container (bowl) emerge tea mixture, remaining water, oj, lemonade and whiskey, stir until fully dissolved
4. Place in freezer for 36 hrs.
5. Serve in glasses — scrape frozen mixture.

Iced Lemonade Tea

INGREDIENTS

6 tea bags
1gal water (sorry, can't read–looks like "Bing")
1 can (6 oz) frozen lemonade
2 qts cold water
¼ cup sugar

DIRECTIONS

Steep tea bags in water for 15 minutes. Add lemonade.
Stir in cold water and sugar. Chill.

NOTES

Contributed by Tricia Clapp

Here's what's cookin' *Iced Lemonade Tea* Serves 8 3
Recipe from the kitchen of *Peg C.* Betty Crocker Outdoor
4/17/81

6 Tea Bags
1 qt Boiling water
1 can 6 oz frz. lemon.
2 qts cold water
1 1/4 c. sugar
Steep tea bags in boiling water
15 min. add lemonade.
Stir in cold water/sugar
chill. —

(over)

Linda's Helpful Hints

I love *Helpful Hints!* I love them for food, throughout the house, the yard, for cleaning, etc. I have a box full of them and am dazzled when they really help!

Peeling hard boiled eggs: boil eggs with 2 Tbsp of white vinegar, then before pouring out water, add a Tbsp of baking soda or cream of tartar. Wait a few minutes and pour out, then cool water and rinse.

Peeling potatoes: soak potatoes in salted cold water before peeling.

Fluffy eggs: Add a tsp of baking powder for every 4 eggs you are making. Beat together before cooking.

Keeping veggies fresh: wrap each in foil (wash and dry before wrapping).

Bacon: this works! Sprinkle flour onto bacon before cooking. Helps keep bacon super crispy and not shrivel.

Gravy consistency: Use rice water instead of plain water.

Sweet Potatoes: Very important – put a pat of butter on sliced potatoes before baking (keeps them moist).

Keep freshly baked cookies fresh: wrap in tissue paper, then store in a container.

Ripening Hachiya persimmons: (the pointy kind). Marcel Matley told me to avoid the astringency of these persimmons by leaving them in the freezer overnight. It mimics the fruit going through a freeze.

Contributed by Linda Larson

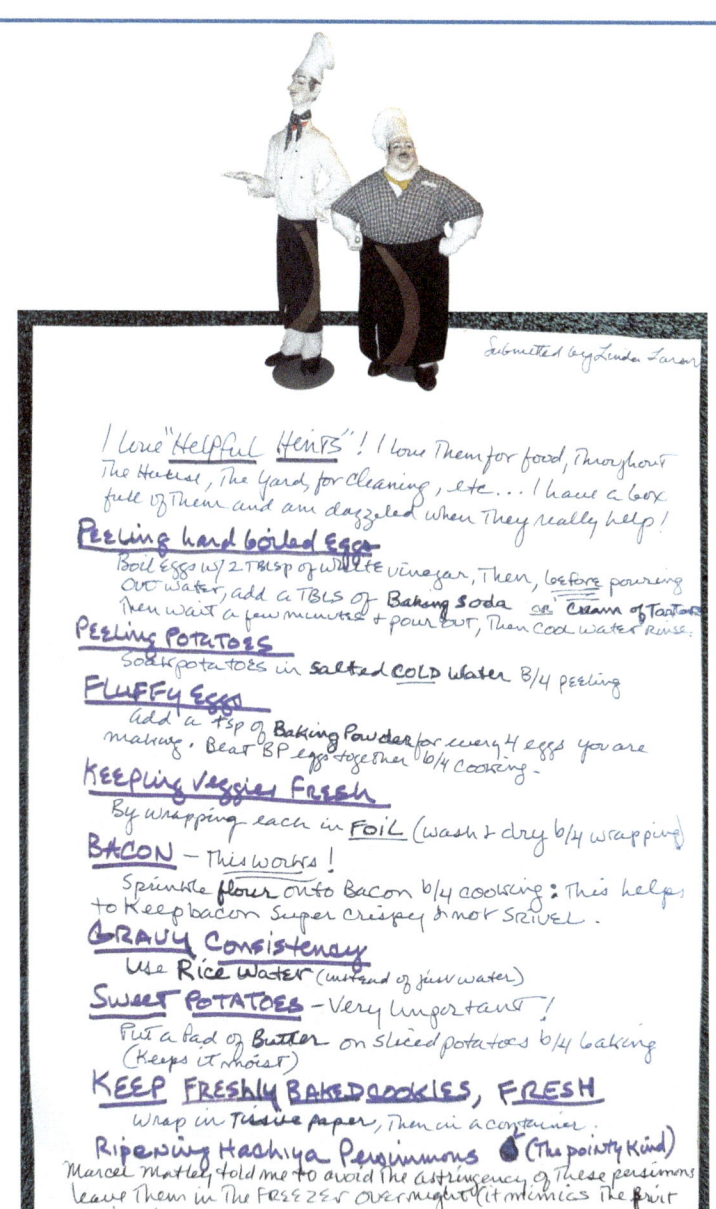

Submitted by Linda Larson

I love "Helpful HINTS"! I love them for food, throughout the House, the yard, for cleaning, etc... I have a box full of them and am dazzled when they really help!

PEELING hard boiled Eggs
Boil eggs w/ 2 TBLSP of WHITE vinegar, then, before pouring out water, add a TBLS of Baking Soda _or_ Cream of Tartar. Then wait a few minutes + pour out, then cool water rinse.

PEELING POTATOES
Soak potatoes in salted COLD Water b/4 peeling

FLUFFY Eggs
Add a tsp of Baking Powder for every 4 eggs you are making. Beat BP + eggs together b/4 cooking -

KEEPING veggies FRESH
By wrapping each in FOIL (wash + dry b/4 wrapping)

BACON — This works !
Sprinkle flour onto Bacon b/4 cooking: This helps to keep bacon super crispy & not shrivel.

GRAVY Consistency
Use Rice Water (instead of just water)

SWEET POTATOES — Very Important !
Put a pad of Butter on sliced potatoes b/4 baking (Keeps it moist)

KEEP FRESHLY BAKED COOKIES, FRESH
Wrap in Tissue paper, then in a container.

Ripening Hashiya Persimmons (The pointy Kind)
Marcel Matley told me to avoid the astringency of these persimmons leave them in the FREEZER overnight (it mimics the fruit going through a FREEZE).

Image Credits

Most photographs in this book were obtained from royalty-free image libraries including Pixabay, Pexels, and Unsplash, and are used in accordance with their respective licenses. These images are intended to *represent* the recipes and themes within this collection, and *may not depict the exact finished dishes*.

Where individual photographers are known, full credit is given on the corresponding recipe page.

All handwritten recipe pages are reproduced with the kind permission of their contributors.

Also Published by Write Choice Ink

The Power of the Pen, AHAF Anthology

Advanced Studies in Handwriting Psychology
(multi-author series)

Advanced Studies in Handwriting Psychology: Sheila Lowe

Advanced Studies in Handwriting Psychology: Jeanette Farmer

Advanced Studies in Handwriting Psychology: Renate Griffiths

*Advanced Studies in Handwriting Psychology: Terry Henley,
June Canoles, Renate Griffiths*

Advanced Studies in Handwriting Psychology: Sr. June Canoles

Advanced Studies in Handwriting Psychology: Roger Rubin

Books by Shirl Solomon
Graphic Sex: Shirl Solomon

Knowing Your Child Through His Handwriting & Drawings

My Name Isn't Rufus

Small Deception

The Fifth Child

Books by Sheila Lowe

Fiction
Poison Pen

Written in Blood

Dead Write

Last Writes

Inkslingers Ball

Outside the Lines
Written Off
Dead Letters
Maximum Pressure
Danger Between the Lines

Beyond the Veil Paranormal Series

What She Saw
Proof of Life
The Last Door

Nonfiction by Sheila Lowe

Reading Between the Lines: Decoding Handwriting
Advanced Studies in Handwriting Psychology
The Complete Idiot's Guide to Handwriting Analysis
Personality & Anxiety in Handwriting

Memoir
Growing From the Ashes

Write Choice Ink is dedicated to publishing works that explore the connection between language, personality, and the written word. And the fiction works of Sheila Lowe

www.sheilalowebooks.com

www.sheilalowe.com